Nickname: Flower of Evil

呼び名は悪の花

THE ABE SADA STORY

Kristine Ohkubo

Please visit: kstoneohkubo.wixsite.com/author

Printed in the United States

Book Layout ©2017 BookDesignTemplates.com

Cover design by Ken Lao/Alchemia Design

Nickname: Flower of Evil/Kristine Ohkubo. —1st ed.

ISBN 978-0-578-55147-0

THIS BOOK IS dedicated to all the women who have stood on their own and persevered as the world around them changed— in some ways, for the worse, to all of the damsels in distress, the persecuted maidens, and the princesses in jeopardy who chose to save themselves without the fabled princes or the knights in shining armor.

ACKNOWLEDGEMENTS

WRITING IS A journey of discovery, and traveling down one path can often lead to many new adventures after the initial voyage. In 2016, I embarked on a journey called *The Sun Will Rise Again*. That period of discovery yielded another project called *Asia's Masonic Reformation*. This book, my most recent undertaking, stemmed from that adventure.

As I continue to travel down this road of discovery and authorship, I would like to acknowledge those individuals who have helped me make the impossible possible by urging me to pursue my dreams on a daily basis.

Along the way, I have relied on countless individuals who have read, offered comments, and assisted in the editing, translating, proofreading, and the design of this book. To each and every one, I would like to extend my infinite heartfelt gratitude.

Lastly, I would like to express my appreciation to Mickey Ohkubo, who helped by verifying my Japanese to English translations. He, without hesitation, provides the bridge between the two worlds in which I exist. 有難うございます。

"Si le viol, le poison, le poignard, l'incendie,
N'ont pas encor brodé de leurs plaisants dessins
Le canevas banal de nos piteux destins,
C'est que notre âme, hélas! N'est pas assez hardie."

If rape, poison, dagger, fire,
Have still not embroidered their pleasant designs
On the banal canvas of our pitiable destinies,
It's because our soul, alas! Is not bold enough.

-- Charles Baudelaire
Les Fleurs du mal/The Flowers of Evil (1857)
Au Lecteur (To the Reader)

Contents

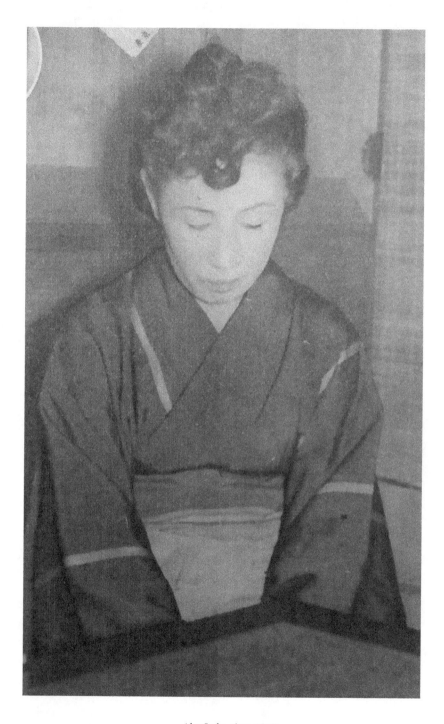

Abe Sada, circa 1947

"She is a slut and a whore. And as what she has done makes clear, she is a woman whom men should fear."

— *Kasahara Kinnosuke (Interrogation, 1936)*

Introduction

WHEN JAPAN TRANSITIONED from 264 years of rule under the military-led Tokugawa Shogunate (1603 to 1867) to the restoration of imperial power during the Meiji era, it embarked on a path of rapid modernization. This period produced dramatic changes in the country's political, social, and economic institutions.

In the years that followed, Japan grew and evolved at an unprecedented rate, and its economy soared to levels that were previously unwitnessed in Asia. However, in a society that had historically been structured around a strict social hierarchy, the cost of this immense growth was primarily borne by its underclass—the women.[1]

Once the shift of power took place, the Shogunate's economy was restructured and its land tax system was reformed. Those who had paid taxes previously were issued certificates of ownership, but common lands became the property of the central government. Under the new law, taxes were paid in cash based on the value of the land rather than the value of the crops grown on the land.[2] Utilizing the taxes collected from individual landholders, the new government invested heavily in industries such as silk and cotton production, railways, and mining. Japan's industrial revolution created a critical need for laborers. The majority of the industrial workforce came from the rural farmlands.[3]

The women who once helped their families on the farm were redirected to work in the factories. By 1900, 250,000 women worked in the textile industry.[4] A little over a decade later that number swelled to an estimated 800,000.[5]

These rural women were often underage, underpaid, and indentured to the factory owners. Indentured labor was not a new concept in Japan. Dating as far back as 1543, when the Portuguese first set foot in the country, a large scale slave trade had existed in which the Portuguese purchased Japanese as slaves and sold them overseas. This practice lasted throughout the sixteenth and seventeenth centuries.[6] The Portuguese also purchased large numbers of Japanese women to bring back to Portugal for sexual purposes.[7] Some of the Japanese women were sold as concubines to the Portuguese, lascar, and African crewmembers serving aboard the Portuguese vessels engaged in trading with Japan.[8]

Dom Sebastian I, the king of Portugal from 1557 to 1578, feared that the slave trade was having a negative impact on Catholic proselytization in Japan and ordered that the practice be banned in 1571.[9]

Toyotomi Hideyoshi, the Imperial Regent, was disgusted by the fact that his people were being sold en masse into slavery. On July 24, 1587, he wrote a letter to Jesuit Vice-Provincial Gaspar Coelho. Coelho was a Jesuit missionary who replaced Francisco Cabral as the Superior and Vice-Provincial of the Jesuit mission in Japan during the late sixteenth century. In his letter Hideyoshi demanded that the Portuguese, Siamese, and Cambodians stop purchasing and enslaving Japanese people and return them to Japan. He blamed the Portuguese and the Jesuits for the slave trade and as a result banned Christian proselytizing altogether.[10]

In 1595 Portugal passed a law banning Chinese and Japanese slavery, but various forms of indentured labor still existed.[11]

Upon being recruited by the textile mills, the women's families were paid a sum of money which they could apply toward paying off loans and defraying the cost of their living expenses. In reality, however, these advance payments were loans from the factory owners that the women were obligated to pay back. A typical contract lasting five to seven years would enable a family to receive an advance payment of ¥200 to ¥300.[12]

On average, women working in the silk mills in 1875 were earning approximately ¥9 annually. By 1880, that figure nearly doubled. Wages were paid annually and the factories deducted an installment from these wages as a repayment for the advances that had been paid to the workers' families.[13]

The women typically worked under grueling conditions and labored twelve to fourteen hours a day. They were often subjected to punishment by the factory inspectors. The punishment came in the form of fines and/or physical abuse and were applied to those women who appeared to have slowed down the production line or who seemed to be inattentive.[14]

Further, the women were confined to company-owned dormitories where their day-to-day lives were governed by strict rules and regulations. The sanitary conditions in these dormitories were deplorable due to a lack of sufficient bathing and laundering facilities. Most of the dormitories were breeding grounds for lice and bedbugs, which aided to the spread of disease.

As a result, tuberculosis was on the rise in Japan during this period, particularly in the rural areas. The women would often contract the disease in the dormitories and infect others that they came in contact with after they returned to their villages to recuperate. Until the 1920s, tuberculosis was responsible for 40% of the deaths of the women living in factory dormitories and 70% of the deaths of the women who had returned to their villages.[15]

Thiamine deficiency (also known as beriberi), a condition that causes disorders of the cardiovascular system and the nervous system, was also common during this period due to the poor diet the women were subjected to.

Many of the women attempted to run away from the factories, but they were chased down, captured, and returned to the factory owners. Several women committed suicide.

Due to their rural background, most of the workers were uneducated. By the 1900s many companies began to offer primary education to their female workforce, but this education was focused on learning skills that could later be utilized by the factories.

After the textile industry, the second largest employer of women during the Industrial Revolution was the sex industry. Prostitution was legalized by the Tokugawa Shogunate in 1617, and fathers had the right to sell their daughters to brothels.

Many families facing poverty, famine, and crop failure often resorted to selling their daughters to brothels in an effort to ease the family's financial burdens. However, selling women to the brothels was not limited only to the families who were financially destitute. The affluent samurai families had established the practice of selling daughters whom they deemed to be sexually promiscuous to the brothels as a form of punishment.

During the Tokugawa (or Edo) period, the practice of infanticide as a form of population control had become prevalent in Japan. Farmers killed their second or third sons soon after birth in what was known as *mabiki*. Mabiki is an agricultural term used to describe the act of pulling plants from an overcrowded garden.

In northern Japan alone, between 60,000 and 70,000 cases of mabiki were recorded each year. Daughters were often spared, because they could be married off, or sold as servants, prostitutes, or geishas.[16]

In 1842, the Shogunate banned induced abortions in Edo (Tokyo), but the law did not extend to the rest of the country until 1869. During the Meiji period, the government strived to promote a larger population in order to exercise greater military and political power in the world arena. The Meiji reformers enacted Japan's first penal code in 1880, which criminalized both abortion and infanticide.[17] An increase in the number of children being born in Japan during the Meiji period contributed to the number of males who could be inducted into the military and the number of females who could be sold to the sex industry.

Despite the legalization of the sex industry, the social attitudes to prostitutes did not change; many Japanese found it easier to blame the victim rather than the society that created the conditions for prostitution to exist.

In 1872, the Meiji government passed the Prostitution Emancipation Act as a response to foreign criticism of Japan's sex trade. The new law freed geishas and prostitutes from being bound by contracts of indentured servitude. However, the law also left many women unemployed. With nowhere else to work, they returned to the brothels under similar contracts. The brothels had relabeled themselves as *kashi zashiki gyo* (room rental establishments).

Three years after the Prostitution Emancipation Act was passed, the government backtracked and once again recognized the legality of contracts of indenture for prostitutes.[18]

Many major cities in Japan allocated specific districts on their outskirts to the sex industry. In 1883, there were 3,156 registered prostitutes in approximately 400 districts. By 1904, that number rose to 43,134. In the next two decades, the number increased to 52,325.[19]

The rapid industrialization of Japan created a largely disproportionate ratio of men to women in the factory areas which fostered the growth of the sex industry.

Women boiling cocoons and reeling silk at a silk factory in Maebashi, Gunma
Prefecture, circa 1900

In the 1890s, the Meiji reformers instituted a state-sponsored education system and along with the Home Ministry introduced the twin ideals of *ryosai kenbo* (good wife, wise mother). These ideals were carried over from the Tokugawa period, when women of the samurai class were considered catalysts for bringing either respect or shame to their families and to their clans. Samurai women were expected to be good examples of propriety and virtue to the members of their household as well as all other members of their clan. They were charged with serving their husbands well by bearing children for them and preserving the honor and lineage of their families. Women were discouraged from forming friendships or becoming intimate with anyone other than those individuals to whom they were introduced to by their parents or by middlemen acting on behalf of their parents.[20]

However, the ideals of modesty, frugality, and purity embodied in ryosai kenbo were reserved primarily for the upper- and middle-class women; the lower-class women, who remained largely uneducated, were simply viewed as laborers required for the factories.[21]

Although women endured repression and hierarchical subjugation during the Tokugawa period, it wasn't until the implementation of the Japanese *Mimpo* (civil code) in 1898 that the subordinate status of women in society was formalized in the law. The new law not only deprived married women of their economic independence, it also further subjected them to the will of the head of the household.[22]

Overall, the extent to which women could participate in society differed over time and in accordance to their social class. In eighth century Japan, it was permissible for women to rule. During the twelfth century, women were allowed to inherit property in their own names. This gave them a degree of freedom and considerable power over their lives. Furthermore, divorce and remarriage were not stigmatized. However, as a result of closer adherence to Confucianism and Buddhism coupled with the advent of samurai culture, the role of women in Japanese society was downgraded to a state of acquiescent confinement.

Beginning with the Tokugawa period and well into the Meiji period, when Japan embraced change and modernization, the social status of women drastically declined. The condition of the lower classes consisting of the impoverished rural women, the factory laborers, and the sex industry workers remained largely unchanged throughout the first half of the twentieth century.

Despite the benefits it gained, the industrial development of Japan came at an enormous cost to Japanese society. The system blatantly exploited the already repressed members of society—its women.

Abe Sada was born in Tokyo's Kanda ward on May 28, 1905 (Meiji era). She was the seventh of eight children born to a family of *tatami* (straw mat) makers. She was raised amidst and forced to find a way to survive in a newly modernized, male-dominated, and misogynistic society.

Tokyo, circa 1905

Key Dates

1336-1573   Kyoto becomes the center of prostitution in Japan during the Muromachi period. [23]

1521-1546   The twelfth Ashikaga Shogun, Yoshihiru, creates a bureau of prostitution to increase government funds and save it from bankruptcy. This act is the first step taken towards licensing prostitution in Japan.[24]

1603   The Tokugawa Shogunate, the feudal Japanese military government, comes to power. The Tokugawa period begins.

1617   The Tokugawa Shogunate issues an order to restrict prostitution to specific areas on the outskirts of cities (*yukaku*).

Prostitutes and courtesans are licensed (*yujo*) and ranked according to hierarchy.

Yoshiwara (the licensed prostitution quarter of Edo/Tokyo) is established near Nihonbashi by Jinemon Shouji.

1640   The Shimabara district in Kyoto is designated as a courtesans' district (similar to Yoshiwara).

1657   On March 2 the Great fire of Meireki destroys 60-70% of Edo (later called Tokyo).

The Yoshiwara quarter is moved to the area adjacent to Asakusa and called *Shin* (New) Yoshiwara.

1853	The Perry Expedition led by Commodore Matthew Perry arrives in Japan.
1854	February 13 – Perry returns to Japan.
	March 31 - The Convention of Kanagawa is signed opening the ports of Shimoda and Hakodate to American ships.
1866	The fifteenth and last Shogun, Tokugawa Yoshinobu, assumes power.
1867	November 9 – Tokugawa Yoshinobu tenders his resignation to the Emperor and formally steps down ten days later, relinquishing governing power to the Emperor.
1868	January 3 – The new imperial government is formed.
	January 27- The Boshin War begins.
	July 4 – The Battle of Ueno takes place.
	October 23 – The reign of Emperor Meiji officially begins.
1869	June 27 – The Boshin War ends.
1870	Japan's Industrial Revolution begins.
1871	The Ministry of Education is established and institutes a school system based closely on the American model.

1872	The Prostitution Emancipation Act is passed.
1877	The Satsuma Rebellion takes place from January 29 to September 24.
1894	The First Sino-Japanese War begins. The war ends in 1895, and for the first time, regional dominance in East Asia shifts from China to Japan.
1898	On July 16, The Civil Code of Japan is implemented.
1904	The Russo-Japanese War begins.
1905	Abe Sada is born in Tokyo.
1912	On July 30 the Meiji Emperor passes away. The Taisho era begins with the reign of the new emperor.
1914	On July 28, World War I begins.

On August 23, Japan declares war on Germany. |
| 1923 | On September 1, The Great Kanto Earthquake devastates Tokyo, Yokohama, and the surrounding prefectures of Chiba, Kanagawa, and Shizuoka, and causes widespread damage throughout the Kanto region. |
| 1926 | On December 25, the Taisho Emperor passes away. The Showa era begins with the reign of the new emperor. |

1931	Japan invades Manchuria.
1936	On February 26, an attempted coup d'état called Ni Ni-Roku Jiken takes place.
	On May 18, the Abe Sada incident takes place.
	From August 1-16 Japan competes at the Summer Olympics in Berlin, Germany.
1937	Second Sino-Japanese War begins.
1940	The 2,600th anniversary of the foundation of Japan is observed and celebrated.
1941	Japan attacks Pearl Harbor, and the Pacific War begins.
1945	Japan surrenders following the atomic bombings of Hiroshima and Nagasaki.
	The Allied Occupation of Japan begins.
	On August 23, The Recreation and Amusement Association is formed to organize brothels to serve the Allied armed forces occupying Japan.
1946	On January 21, the Supreme Commander for the Allied Powers abolishes the licensed prostitution system.
	In November a new *akasen* (red line) system is introduced under which licensed nightlife establishments are permitted to offer sexual

services under the guise of being an ordinary club or café. This is followed by the establishment of the "blue line" system under which it becomes permissible to offer sexual services under the guise of being restaurants, bars, or other less strictly-regulated establishments.

1947   Imperial Ordinance No. 9 is passed making it punishable by law to entice women to act as prostitutes. (Prostitution itself remains legal.)

1956   On May 24, the Diet passes the Anti-Prostitution Law.

1958   In April, the Anti-Prostitution Law becomes effective.

Yoshiwara, circa 1872

CHAPTER I

Abe no Kazoku

"While I was being brought up my family was prospering as it never had before. We always had six craftsmen in the house, and when they got busy they hired as many as ten or fifteen. We were wealthy and as the youngest child my parents spoiled me."

-Abe Sada (Interrogation, 1936)[25]

LITTLE IS KNOWN about Sada's father, Abe Shigeyoshi. He was born in Chiba prefecture in 1853, the year of the Perry Expedition.

The Perry Expedition was not the first U.S. delegation to visit Japan. Since 1790, approximately twenty-seven U.S. ships had visited Japan, only to be turned away. In 1851, the U.S. Secretary of State authorized Commodore John H. Aulick, commander of the East India Squadron, to attempt to return seventeen shipwrecked Japanese to their country, hoping that the act of goodwill would make the Japanese more receptive to trade with the United States. On May 10, 1851, American President Millard Fillmore signed a letter addressed to the Emperor of Japan requesting friendship and commerce. The letter was to be delivered to the Emperor by Aulick; however,

Aulick was relieved of his command and replaced by Commodore Matthew Calbraith Perry.

When Perry arrived in Japan, he was determined to force an end to the country's 220-year-old policy of seclusion and open her ports to American trade. He threatened to do so by force if necessary.

Under threat, the Japanese government acquiesced and the Convention of Kanagawa was signed on March 31, 1854, opening Japanese ports for trade with American merchants.[26] The years following the signing of the treaty were marked by great turmoil, resulting in the Shogun's fall from power. The emperor gained formal control of the country during the Meiji Restoration of 1868, and Japan embarked on a path of swift change and modernization.

It is difficult to determine how this rapidly changing society may have impacted Shigeyoshi and his biological family, or to know for certain what their financial circumstances were. What is known is that Shigeyoshi was ultimately adopted by the Abe family to help them with their tatami business, and later became their heir.

Shigeyoshi's adoptive father was a fourth generation tatami maker who had inherited the family business from his father.[27] Whether Shigeyoshi's adoption took place when he was a child or an adult is unknown. The practice of adopting an adult male as an heir to the family business was a common practice in Japan back in those days, and it continues even today.

The process known as *yoshi-engumi* (adoption of an heir) became popular among the samurai class during the Tokugawa period. The samurai class would adopt sons for the purpose of retaining their strong and influential position in society. For the adoptees, yoshi-engumi provided a means to ascend the social ladder by shedding their second-born status and assuming roles as the heads of households and the owners of family businesses.

Sometimes, a family would adopt a daughter's husband as their heir. The adopted son-in-law was known as the *mukoyoshi* (adopted husband). Oftentimes, he would change his last name to his wife's family name and become the head of the household.

Another common form of adoption involved adopting both adult men and women. If a potential adoptee was already married, the married couple would be adopted together.

Adoptions did not merely take place in situations where a family was childless. In some cases, the existing male heir was not a viable choice to inherit the business and assume leadership of the household, prompting the family to look elsewhere.

As with many of the customs associated with the elite class during the Tokugawa period, the practice of yoshi-engumi was eventually adopted by others who ranked lower on the social ladder.[28]

Although the caste system in Japan was formally abolished in 1871, barriers to the true integration of the classes still existed. The *mibunsei* (identity system) was created during Japan's feudal period to help bring stability to the country.

The system of strict customs and regulations was based on Confucianism, the philosophical and ethical teachings which characterized traditional Chinese society. Confucianism was introduced in Japan during the sixth century and gained acceptance after Prince Shotoku Taishi enacted the *Jushichijokenpo* (Seventeen Article Constitution) in 604 CE. The Constitution established Confucian ideals and Buddhist ethics as the moral foundations of the Japanese nation. During the Tokugawa era, there was a revival of Confucian ethics after the introduction of Neo-Confucianism. Neo-Confucianism represented the moral, ethical, and metaphysical Chinese philosophy that synthesized Taoist cosmology and Buddhist spirituality with the core Confucian principles focused on society and government. Neo-Confucianism originated in China during the Tang dynasty (681-907).

MIBUNSEI

Emperor

Court Nobles

Shogun

Daimyo

Shi (Samurai)

Nō (Peasants)

Kō (Artisans)

Shō (Merchants)

Eta and Hinin

The social ranking system during Japan's feudal period

Figure1

The mibunsei consisted of the emperor, the court nobles, the shogun, and the daimyo (feudal lords who were landowners and vassals of the shogun) comprising the upper tier of the social hierarchy. Below them, the population was divided into *shinokosho* (four classes): *shi* (samurai), *no* (farming peasants), *ko* (artisans), and *sho* (merchants). The merchants were ranked below the peasants in this system because they generated wealth without producing any products.

People who did not fall into the four classes were considered to be outcasts and untouchables. They were shunned, ostracized, segregated into separate communities, and forced to wear special clothing and hairstyles which signaled their status to others. One group was known as the *eta* (pollution abundant) because they worked in occupations condemned by Shinto and Buddhist traditions. This group included butchers, executioners, and leather tanners. The other group was known as the *hinin* (non-human), and included actors, convicted criminals, prostitutes, and courtesans. Hence, the social classes in Japan were not necessarily arranged by wealth, but by what Asian philosophers described as moral purity.

This adherence to moral purity brings into question the ranking of the samurai class, which constituted about 7–8% of the population. A samurai's job involved killing and should certainly have relegated them into the group of outcasts; however, this was not the case. Even the *ronin* (the master-less samurai), who were generally afforded very low levels of respect, had no income, and often became gamblers, bandits, or participated in other similar occupations, were still ranked at the top of the shinokosho.

While Abe Shigeyoshi's past seems somewhat ambiguous, the family history of Sada's mother, Abe Katsu, is just as vague. She was one of four daughters raised by a single mother after her father was killed during the Battle of Ueno in 1868.

The Battle of Ueno was a clash between the elite corps of the Shogun known as the *shogitai* and the Imperial Army (the *Kangun*) during the Boshin War. The struggle took place on July 4, 1868.

The fighting was primarily confined to an area near Toeizan Kan'ei-ji Endon-in, an important Tokugawa family temple, and the Nezu Shrine. Katsu's father was a civilian who managed a money lending business in Ueno. It is not known how he came to be slashed to death during the battle.[29]

It is also not clear how Katsu met her future husband, Shigeyoshi. It is quite possible that theirs was an arranged marriage, commonly referred to as an *omiai* in Japan.

Omiai was the practice of matchmaking, which began in twelfth century Japan. During that time, marriage was simply an agreement between two families and the children did not have the option to choose their own spouses. The practice was popular among the elite as it enabled families to preserve their bloodlines and social status. [30] Later, during the Tokugawa period, omiai was practiced by the classes further down the social hierarchy who were trying to emulate samurai customs.

William Johnston, the author of *Geisha, Harlot, Strangler, Star: A Woman, Sex, and Morality in Modern Japan*, speculated that the Abe family may have been childless and may have adopted Shigeyoshi and Katsu as their son and daughter. Shigeyoshi and Katsu in turn may have decided to carry on the tatami-making business and the family line as a couple.[31]

The couple conceived eight children together, of whom only four survived until adulthood. Two of the Abe boys died in 1915. One son succumbed to typhus and the other died of heart failure as a result of thiamine deficiency (beriberi). Another boy died soon after birth. Of the children that survived, Sada was the youngest. Her brother, Shintaro, was nineteen years older. The second eldest child was a daughter named Toku, who was eighteen years older than Sada. The third oldest was also a girl named Teruko, who was seven years older.

The family's tatami business and residence were located on Shingin-cho 99 in the Kanda ward, one of Tokyo's 35 wards prior to 1947. Shingin-cho's residents consisted primarily of carpenters, roofers, plasterers, and craftsman.[32] The Abes also owned several rental properties throughout the city.

As the oldest son, Shintaro was expected to inherit the tatami business; however, he had been disowned by his parents. Instead, Toku, the second oldest child, was made the successor and her husband was chosen to carry on the Abe family business. The Abes had adopted a craftsman named Imao Seitaro who later became Toku's husband.

Shintaro was a womanizer and the focus of ongoing domestic troubles for some time. He frequently brought home women he had met at various bars and restaurants where the women were employed. He eventually married a geisha named Kurokawa Ume. The couple repeatedly gave Toku and her husband Seitaro a difficult time due to the inheritance issue. The Abe family's troubles worsened in 1922, when Shintaro and Ume ran off and took the family's savings with them.

Teruko was described as a sexually promiscuous girl, having begun an affair with a local craftsman when she was still relatively young. Despite the morality imposed on young women at the time, she was still able to get married. Unfortunately, the marriage did not last long, and shortly after leaving her husband Teruko took on several lovers. This angered her father so much that he resorted to selling her to a brothel. Friends and family were shocked and pleaded with him to buy her back. Teruko was eventually brought back home, but the experience had changed her. She settled into a quiet life, and in time she married a tatami maker from Ikebukuro named Tatsumi Toshisaburo.[33]

CHAPTER II

Growing Up in Kanda

"My mother liked garish things and was very vain."

-Abe Sada (Interrogation, 1936)[34]

IN 1889, TOKYO consisted of fifteen wards. In 1932, large areas from five surrounding districts were merged into the city and reorganized to form twenty new wards, bringing the total number of special wards in Tokyo to thirty-five. Kanda was one of Tokyo's fifteen original wards. After 1947, the number of wards in Tokyo was reduced to twenty-three, and Kanda was merged with Kojimachi to form the modern-day Chiyoda ward.

Together with Nihonbashi and Kyobashi, Kanda formed the core of Shitamachi, the original downtown center of Edo (Tokyo). [35] Shitamachi and Yamanote were the traditional names for two areas of Tokyo otherwise known as lower and upper Tokyo, respectively. Although Yamanote was comprised of the hilly part of Tokyo and Shitamachi was physically the low, marshy part of the city located along the Sumida River and extending further east, the identity of the two areas was based more on culture and caste rather than actual geography. The affluent, upper-class residences were located in Yamanote while the merchants' and artisans' residences and shops were located in Shitamachi.[36]

When Sada was born, Abe Shigeyoshi was already 52 years old and consequently did not spend much time with his daughter as she was growing up. His wife, on the other hand, doted on Sada and instilled in her a love for flashy clothes and makeup, which is something she herself was known to be particularly fond of. Katsu attempted to live her life through her daughter and raised her child by allowing her to have practically anything that she desired. She was proud of her daughter's beauty and often dressed her up and paraded her around in public.

When Sada was six years old, she began taking singing and shamisen lessons, the mastery of which was often associated with the geisha culture in those days. Contrary to the Western interpretation which equates a geisha with a prostitute, geishas have traditionally been entertainers who possess long cultivated talents in the areas of dancing, singing, and the art of conversation. Although historically there have been instances where geisha were engaged in selling sexual services, it was never a widely accepted part of a geisha's role.

The geisha culture first originated in thirteenth century Japan and was very different from what we know today. The first geishas were actually men known as *houkan* or *taikomochi*. They were entertainers who also served as attendants to the daimyo.[37]

By the sixteenth century, the male geisha's role had evolved into that of a storyteller known as an *otogishu* or *hanashishu*. These men were highly skilled in storytelling, humor, and conversation. They were also confidents and advisors to the daimyo and took part in battles alongside their masters.[38]

During the seventeenth century, when Japan had entered a period of peace, the role of the storytellers and advisors changed once again and they became entertainers only. Some worked alongside the *oiran* (the high-class Japanese courtesans who resided in the pleasure quarters of Edo, Kyoto, and other major cities during the Tokugawa period).[39]

In 1751, the first female geishas emerged and by the end of the eighteenth century, the female entertainers outnumbered their male counterparts. Eventually, the female geishas began to lure business away from the oiran as more and more patrons preferred the sophistication and artistic skills the geishas possessed.[40]

By the 1920s, however, the popularity of the geishas declined due to the arrival of the *jokyuu* (café girls and showgirls). This new profession originated in Tokyo and was less time consuming to join compared to other types of unskilled labor or apprenticeship positions. The café girls were able to earn a sizeable salary in those days, making the job highly attractive to young girls from Japan's rural countryside. Unlike the geisha, the jokyuu entered the profession without a debt to her employer, and she was free to quit her job at any time.[41]

As the youngest child, Sada was extremely spoiled and she disliked going to school. With the exception of earning the top grade for music she received relatively poor grades in elementary school. Her teachers urged her to give up her shamisen lessons and focus on her school work, but Sada and her mother would not hear of it. Soon her music lessons became her primary focus.

After graduating from Akiyoshi Elementary School, Sada's parents hired private tutors to teach her sewing and calligraphy. During the late 1800s and early 1900s, women were expected to master domestic skills such as sewing and cooking, as well as develop the moral and intellectual skills to raise strong, intelligent sons for the sake of the nation. These skills were also considered necessary for any woman hoping to marry a reputable man. Naturally, Sada continued with her singing and shamisen lessons as well.[42]

It was during this time when the domestic troubles with Sada's older brother, Shintaro, were escalating. Sada's parents wanted to spare her from having to witness the quarrelling and often sent her out of the house to play. Consequently, Sada spent a great deal of time away from home and unsupervised.

She soon became friends with other boys and girls from her neighborhood who also enjoyed the same level of freedom. One of those friends was Fukuda Minako. Sada and Minako spent a great deal of time together and it was through her that Sada became acquainted with an older Keio University student named Sakuragi Ken. Ken was a friend of Minako's older brother and it wasn't long before he and Sada became friendly with one other. Sada was fifteen years old at the time.

One summer day while Sada and Ken were playing around on the second floor of Minako's house, he took the play a little too far and forced Sada to have sexual intercourse with him. Confused, frightened, and bleeding badly after the experience, Sada told her mother about what had happened. A few days later Sada met Ken again and explained to him that she had told her mother everything. She urged him to tell his parents what had happened as well. However, Ken refused to do so and he stopped coming to Minako's house. Sada's mother went to the Sakuragi house to speak with Ken's parents, but they refused to speak with someone from the lower part of Tokyo.[43] Many years after the incident, Sada stated, "At the time I didn't think that I wanted to marry that student, but I couldn't stand to think that he was making a fool out of me the whole time."[44]

Sada believed that losing her virginity had made it impossible for her to get married. This was at a time when women were classified into two different categories in Japanese society: the women who were pure and became wives and mothers, and the women who became mistresses and prostitutes. For families who aspired to social respectability, a sexually experienced woman was considered an undesirable marriage partner. These families would often hire a private investigator to research the family and personal background of the women their sons wanted to marry. Once it was revealed that a woman was no longer a virgin, it made no difference to the family if the experience arose from rape or sexual promiscuity. Sada felt that it was impossible for her to hide the fact that she was no longer a virgin for the sake of getting married, as her mother had advised her to do. Katsu had told her daughter that the man had taken advantage of her by doing something to her that she didn't understand, so it was nothing to worry about.[45] Furthermore, Sada could not bring herself to discuss the facts about her virginity with a potential marriage partner, so over time she became increasingly confused about what to do and grew extremely bitter.

The incident went unreported to the police since the victim would often face a stigma far worse than the trauma caused by concealing the crime. Oftentimes, Japanese police failed to recognize rape as a serious crime, particularly if it happened to be rape committed by an acquaintance, and the police did not sympathize with the victim.[46]

Sex offense statutes were enacted by the Meiji government in 1907, and to this day they remain unchanged. The law treats sexual assault very lightly, and Japanese men often get away with rape because the police are reluctant to investigate and victims often settle quietly.

The odds that a perpetrator of rape will get arrested and prosecuted in Japan are fairly low. Even if the man is found guilty, there is a good possibility that he will never spend a day in jail for the crime as long as he apologizes and pays for the damages. According to the Ministry of Defense, of the arrests made for sexual assault every year only about half end up being prosecuted. If convicted, the maximum sentence that sexual assault carries is only three years.

The problem is further compounded by the fact that the attitude in the justice system and in Japanese society is to find something or somebody other than the attacker to blame—namely the victim, or more conveniently, alcohol.[47]

For this reason, Sada agonized over the matter. No one seemed to sense her despair over having been categorized as an undesirable marriage partner in a society that only recognized two moral extremes for women.[48] She also grew resentful over the fact that her mother chose to pacify her with material things. After the rape, Katsu bought Sada a new *koto* (a musical instrument) as well as other things and spoiled her even more.[49]

CHAPTER III

Sex Industry Commodity

"But because my parents had abandoned me, I threw myself to the fates and instead of thinking of it as work thought of it as play. I moved from place to place as I saw fit and had no hopes for the future as I worked as a geisha."

-Abe Sada (Interrogation, 1936)[50]

FOLLOWING THE RAPE, Sada's attitude to life changed. Knowing that pursuing a path to a respectable marriage was pointless, she spent more and more time in Asakusa, Tokyo's main entertainment district, with a group of friends she later described as delinquents.

Asakusa, located at the heart of Shitamachi, experienced tremendous growth during the Tokugawa period, thanks in part to the rich *fudasashi* (middlemen) in nearby Kuramae. These men earned a substantial amount of money for storing rice, which was once used as a system of payment. The wealthy fudasashi frequented Asakusa's kabuki theaters and geisha houses. The money they poured into Asakusa propelled it to become a major entertainment center in Tokyo and it featured famous cinemas such as the Denkikan.[51] The Denkikan was the first dedicated movie theater in Japan, established in October, 1903. The theater was originally built to showcase *denki* (electrical) displays and was later converted into a movie theater by the most successful film company in the nation at the time, Yoshizawa Shoten. The theater became the symbol of motion pictures, and many theaters soon emerged throughout Japan bearing the name Denkikan.[52]

Sada's behavior continued to degenerate during this period and she eventually started stealing money from her parents. One day, she stole ¥15 and went to Asakusa with her friends to have a good time. After all the fun had ended, she realized that she had taken too much money, but she did not want to bring any of the remaining money back home. She feared that in doing so, she would be discovered for having committed the theft. Instead, she divided the leftover money among her friends. She learned that having money afforded her a certain level of freedom and respect. Years later, when recalling the times she had spent in Asakusa with her friends, she stated that they treated her magnificently when she bought them meals and drinks, calling her "Saachan." [53] *Chan* is a diminutive honorific suffix used in the Japanese language to express endearment. It is commonly used when referring to babies, young children, close friends, and female adolescents.

All of this took place during the time when Teruko and her first husband were in the process of leaving the house and everything was in disarray. Under the circumstances, Sada's parents ignored her, causing her to become increasingly more disdainful.

Sada's typical day consisted of being served breakfast in bed, after which she would get dressed and go straight to Asakusa. There, she frequented the fashionable restaurants and returned home late at night. Her parents made it very convenient for her to prolong this behavior. Aside from nailing her bedroom door shut once to prevent her from leaving the house, Shigeyoshi pretended not to notice that his youngest daughter was getting dressed up and languishing away at the entertainment district each day. Katsu supported Sada's delinquent behavior by secretly allowing her back into the house when she returned home late at night.[54]

Sada continued to pilfer money from her parents and carried on this way with her delinquent friends for about a year.

That was the year when Teruko left her first husband and returned home to her family. Not long afterwards, she began an illicit affair with a craftsman. Displeased with their daughter's affair, the Abes decided to take the matter into their hands and began making arrangements for her to get married once again. Sada was sixteen years old at the time, and her mother feared that her youngest daughter would expose Teruko's affairs and derail the wedding arrangements. A decision was made to get her out of the way by making her a housemaid.

Sada was taken to the home of an affluent family who resided near the Seishin Joshi Gakuin, a private school for girls founded in 1908, in the Shiba ward. (Shiba was one of the 32 wards of Tokyo which were reorganized in 1947. It was merged with the Akasaka and Azabu wards to form the modern day Minato ward.) There she became the maid to the family's young daughter. However, having been spoiled by her mother practically all of her life, Sada found that life as a maid was unbearable.

Approximately a month into her new role as a maid, she naively decided to put on the daughter's best kimono and ring and visit the Asakusa Kinryukan Theater. In 1918, Japan experienced an opera boom, and Kinryukan was home to the Asakusa Opera.[55] Sada had thought that no harm would come of it as long as she returned the items after her outing. However, things did not play out as she had expected. Teruko came looking for her in Asakusa and immediately returned her to her employers. From there Sada was whisked off to the police station, and this established her police record.

To add to Sada's troubles, Shintaro and Ume encouraged her to become a geisha. They told her that as a geisha she would be able to wear beautiful kimonos and live in luxury. Certainly, Shintaro was motivated entirely by financial gain as he would have earned ¥300 from the geisha house if they accepted his sister. It was easy to put ideas in Sada's naive head as she already had a romantic infatuation with being a geisha without completely understanding what that kind of a lifestyle entailed. She assumed that geishas were simply beautiful women who dressed in expensive kimonos, played the shamisen, sang, danced, and lived in luxury. One night, on an impulse, she ran away to a geisha house in Asakusa. After doing so, she realized that she could not tolerate being away from home and returned the same night.

Not long after, Shintaro and his wife ran off and took the family's entire savings with them. This devastated the Abes, and forced them to sell their tatami-making business and move to the Saitama prefecture where Toku was living with her husband.

Although the Saitama prefecture is Tokyo's neighbor to the north and much of southeastern Saitama is considered a suburb of Tokyo, the western parts of the prefecture are mostly rural and mountainous.

Sada, who had been accustomed to spending her days in Asakusa, did not find rural Saitama to her liking. She started frequenting Western-style restaurants and less reputable establishments on her own and soon became involved with a neighborhood man. Shortly thereafter, the proprietor of a teahouse introduced her to a newspaper reporter with whom she ran off to an inn in Kawasaki. Her parents learned about the incident, tracked her down, and brought her back home. Her father was furious and threatened to sell her off to a brothel, as he had done years earlier to Teruko. Sada later admitted that the prospect of being sold to a brothel frightened her and she begged for her father's forgiveness.

Shigeyoshi did not budge, however, and in 1923 when Sada was still only seventeen years old, he took her to a distant relative's house in Yokohama and asked him to make her a licensed prostitute. Sada did not argue with her father and quietly accepted her fate. She believed that her body was already damaged and there was nothing that she could do about it.

The distant relative was Inaba Masatake, a wood carver who served as a part-time intermediary enabling women to enter geisha houses or brothels for licensed prostitution. He was married to Abe Shintaro's sister-in-law, Kurokawa Hana. Masatake had been the intermediary who provided the introductions for his wife's sisters to gain entrance to the geisha houses. A woman was not permitted to become a geisha or a licensed prostitute on her own; she needed a state-registered intermediary to provide the introduction to an *okiya* (geisha house) or brothel. And if she wanted to transfer to a different geisha house or brothel, she had to rely on the intermediary for that process as well.[56]

Since Sada was still underage, she lived with Masatake and his family for approximately one month before being admitted as an apprentice geisha at the Kanaya okiya. Before long, Sada realized that her image of a geisha had been an unrealistic one and that being the newest apprentice had its challenges. As spoiled as she was, she also found the discipline required of an apprentice geisha intolerable. She asked Masatake to have her transferred to another okiya. Masatake obliged and received an advance of ¥200 for aiding Sada in becoming a full-fledged geisha at the Shunshin Mino okiya located in Yokohama's Naka ward.[57]

As a low-ranked geisha Sada's services were primarily sexual and she came to the realization that she would never ascend to the level of a leading geisha. On the other hand, those geishas who engaged primarily in sex with their clients had a greater monetary value and could command higher advances from the okiya which employed them.

When Sada could no longer put up with life at Shunshin Mino, she approached Masatake once again and asked him to introduce her to another okiya. Naturally, he was more than happy to oblige. He introduced her to a more sexually explicit okiya called Kamochu and received a payment of ¥600 in return.[58]

On September 1, 1923, the Tokyo-Yokohama metropolitan area was struck by a 7.9-magnitude earthquake. The Great Kanto Earthquake, as it came to be known, caused unthinkable damage and resulted in a death toll of over 140,000.[59] The

Kamochu okiya and Masatake's house were among the properties that burned down to the ground from the resulting fires.

Left without a home, Masatake moved his family and Sada to the Toyama prefecture. Unfortunately for Sada, the okiya that were located further away from Tokyo and Kyoto functioned more like brothels than sophisticated entertainment establishments. This was evident from the ¥1,000 advance payment Masatake received for introducing Sada to the Heianro okiya where she began working under the alias of Haruko.[60]

While Sada was living with Masatake in Yokohama, the two had commenced a sexual relationship. Wanting to continue his relationship with her, Masatake rented a house conveniently close to the new okiya where she was working.

Things appeared to be going well at Heianro until Sada was accused of taking items belonging to the other geishas and pawning them for money. The charge was investigated, but she was never formally charged as the owner of the okiya refused to press charges. However, when she stole several shamisen plectrums and a silver pipe and pawned them for ¥50, she was arrested. The police did not actually charge her with the crime, but her arrest made it impossible for her to return to Heianro to work.

In October of 1924, Masatake moved his household to the Shiba ward in Tokyo and took Sada with him. She lived with him without returning to work until May of 1925. It was during this time when Sada, who considered Masatake to be her lover, was disillusioned once again. Masatake used his role as an intermediary to have sexual relationships with the women he had aided. Sada's disillusionment came after realizing that his wife knew of the affairs and did not care. She simply saw the women her husband helped as a source of income and she didn't care if he had sex with them.

Sada decided to distance herself from Masatake and asked that he introduce her to an okiya located in Iida City in the southern Nagano prefecture of the Chubu region of Japan. He obliged, and she began working at an establishment known as

Mikawaya, this time using the alias Seiko. Mikawaya provided Sada with an advance of ¥1,500, which she used to pay off her debts to Masatake. [61]

Years later, Masatake and his wife adopted a young girl named Kumiko. It was rumored that she was the daughter of Masatake and Sada, born in Taisho 14 (1925) when Sada was twenty years old. However, Sada suffered from endometriosis which left her unable to conceive and she was subjected to gynecological examinations as a geisha, so the rumors of a hidden pregnancy were unfounded. It is far more likely that since Masatake worked as in intermediary for young women to get into the geisha houses and the licensed brothels that the girl was the child of someone he had assisted.[62]

During the time Sada worked at the okiya in Iida City, she suffered a nervous breakdown. The okiya's owner found her sitting on the floor in her room pulling her hair out and striking the floor with her legs. A doctor was summoned to the okiya and he diagnosed Sada's condition as hysteria. The following day when one of her regular clients called on her and gave her a watch and ¥30 in cash, she struck him on the head with the watch. Her behavior seemed so extreme that the owner of the okiya and other geishas assumed that Sada might have been abusing intravenous drugs. However, since she did not have any needle marks on her body, they quickly ruled that out as the cause of her deranged outbursts. Soon after the incident, Sada left Mikawaya and never entered another okiya.

Sada's strange behavior could have been the result of the ongoing stress she had endured since being raped, or it could have been a symptom of venereal disease. [63]

Doctor Matthew Tull, an associate professor and the director of anxiety disorders research in the Department of Psychiatry and Human Behavior at the University of Mississippi Medical Center, writes that in many instances the experience of rape or an attempted rape can have a tremendous impact on the victim's life. A person who has been raped will generally experience high levels of distress. For example, the individual may have strong feelings of shame, guilt, anxiety, fear, anger, and sadness. Further, the stigma associated with rape may enhance these feelings. In some individuals, these feelings may subside over time, but others may continue to experience some form of psychological distress for months or years to come.

Survivors of rape have also been found to be high at risk for developing substance abuse disorders, major depression, generalized anxiety disorder, obsessive-compulsive disorder, and eating disorders. The risk of contracting these disorders may be greater for people who have experienced sexual assault at a younger age. Some rape survivors have been observed to engage in risky sexual behaviors or have greater numbers of sexual partners.[64]

Sada was clearly distressed, not only about being taken advantage of by Sakuragi Ken, but also by what she perceived as a lack of understanding and sensitivity from the people closest to her. Her father was far too busy with other matters and he was generally disengaged from her. His involvement was limited to those occasions when he assumed the authoritarian role and elected to discipline Sada by selling her into prostitution. Her mother believed that the best way to deal with the situation was by further spoiling her daughter. Additionally, her parents chose to get her out of the way rather than to deal with her or address what was troubling her directly, first by making her a house maid and later by selling her off to a geisha house.

It was also discovered that Sada had contracted syphilis. Mark Cichocki, a registered HIV/AIDS nurse educator at the University of Michigan's HIV/AIDS Treatment Program and author of the book *Living with HIV: A Patient's Guide*, writes that the signs and symptoms of syphilis are related to the stage of the infection. The first stage involves the appearance of a painless sore on the genitals, rectum, or mouth. After the sore heals, the second stage will usually manifest as a rash. The symptoms of the second stage of syphilis will disappear with or without treatment; however, without treatment, the infection will progress to the third stage. The third stage of syphilis is the latent, or hidden stage. There will not be any noticeable symptoms at this stage, but the bacteria will remain in the body. This stage could last for years before progressing to what is known as tertiary syphilis.

One of the three major complications of tertiary syphilis is neurosyphilis, which affects the central nervous system. Syphilis is no longer contagious during the tertiary stage, but it can lead to seizures, personality changes, hallucinations, dementia, schizophrenia, and stroke.[65]

Sada had worked as a geisha for five years. Until she moved to the Nagano okiya where the geishas were not tested for venereal disease, she had prided herself in not having become a prostitute. But contracting venereal disease ended that illusion. She believed that she had contracted syphilis while working in Nagano.[66]

On New Year's Day in 1927, Sada moved to a licensed brothel called Misonoro located in the Tobita district of Osaka and started working as a prostitute under the name of Sonomaru. This was also the time when she ended her business relationship with Masatake.[67]

The Tobita district or *Tobita Shinchi* covers approximately twelve city blocks and is located in the heart of downtown Osaka. There was another red-light district known as *Otobe Shinchi*, which was home to two thousand prostitutes and one hundred brothels. Although the exact date of its establishment is unknown, Osaka's historical records indicate that impoverished girls from Japan's rural communities and wives fleeing abusive husbands were flocking to the city in search of "work" as early as the late Meiji period (1868-1912).[68] On January 16, 1912, a fire destroyed the area forcing the *yukaku* (brothel) owners to relocate their businesses to the current Tobita district.

Tobita had somewhat of a Bohemian atmosphere during the 1930s. In addition to the working women, there were also a number of artists, musicians, and others who were opposed to the militarization of Japan who called Tobita their home.[69]

Misonoro advanced Sada ¥2,800 and she used part of the money to pay off her debt to the Mikawaya okiya in Nagano.

She also gave ¥200 to ¥300 to her mother as she had been instrumental in finding a new intermediary in Yokohama.

After working at Misonoro for a year, Sada became discouraged once again. She had hoped to drop out of the business of prostitution, but found that she was unable to do so. She moved to another brothel in Osaka called Asahiseki. Although she had passed her time uneventfully at Misonoro, things were about to change.

Within six months of working at Asahiseki, Sada was accused of trying to elope with one of her clients. The situation calmed down and she continued to work at the brothel, but her working relationship became strained again when she started to engage in petty theft. Feeling that Sada had become a liability, the owner went to great lengths to have her transferred to another brothel. She was sent to Tokueiro, where she remained for nearly two years and worked under the alias Sadako.

Sada continued to experience health issues and contracted syphilis once again.[70] Prior to the introduction of penicillin in Japan, syphilis was treated with a drug known as Salvarsan or compound 606. The drug was developed in 1910 by a prominent Japanese bacteriologist, Hata Sahachiro.[71] The diluted drug was both difficult and painful to inject and it did not cure syphilis overnight. Sada had received ten injections when she was first diagnosed with the disease. Syphilis is one of several bacterial sexually transmitted diseases that are relatively easy to catch again, particularly if the individual engages in unprotected sexual activity before the treatment is actually completed.[72]

Sada also became ill with typhus. Scrub typhus occurs in Southeast Asia, Japan, and northern Australia and is spread by chiggers (mites). This means that the brothel where she was working was infested with them, particularly since Japan is prone to hot and humid summers.

After spending nearly two years at Tokueiro, Sada was on the run once again. She reached out to an intermediary who had previously helped her; however, the police had gotten in touch with him informing him that Sada was trying to escape. He responded by returning her to Tokueiro's owner. The owner told Sada that if she had succeeded in running away, he would have taken possession of her parent's rental properties in Tokyo. This threat, whether it was true or not, scared her into submission and she was transferred to another brothel in Osaka's Matsushima district called Miyakoro, where she worked under the alias Azuma. After just two weeks she ran away again, this time to Tokyo. She contacted another intermediary who simply informed Miyakoro of her whereabouts. She was returned to Osaka and transferred to yet another brothel called Taishoro where she assumed the alias Okaru.

Sada was twenty-six years old at the time and conditions at Taishoro were far worse than any other establishment she had worked in before. The owner forced her to walk the streets and pull customers in to the brothel like a common streetwalker.

Eventually, Sada's persistence paid off. She managed to steal ¥100 from a customer and escaped to Kobe. In doing so, she said good-bye to licensed prostitution forever.[73]

CHAPTER IV

Not Suited for a Normal Life

"...he told me that he didn't have a monopoly on me and that I could do whatever I wanted, but that once I started a business I would have to get serious with him. If I had a lover at the time, he told me to tell him about it. If my lover seemed good enough for me, Professor Omiya said that he would act as a go-between for us to get married. After that, he said that he would think of me as his younger sister and would take care of me until he died."

-Abe Sada (Interrogation, 1936)[74]

SADA FACED CONSIDERABLE challenges once she was no longer reliant on the brothel system for her livelihood. While she was living at home and working as a prostitute, she was able to push off the responsibilities of daily life on to others. On her own, she tackled the tasks of shopping, cooking, and cleaning for the first time in her life.

Using the alias Yoshii Masako, she found work as a café hostess. However, still burdened by the advances that she owed to the brothels, she felt that her income as a café hostess was inadequate. She wanted to find a job where she could earn at least ¥100 a month so she approached her customers for help. One of her customers told her that he did have a job that paid well and asked her to accompany him to his place. Even at age twenty-six, Sada was still rather naïve. She was unaware that the customer was a pimp.

Although she had worked as a café hostess for only a short time, she was convinced that she would never be able to earn a decent living working at a regular job. With no other choice, she turned to prostitution once again—this time illegally. Unfortunately for Sada, the pimp exploited her and took all of the money she had earned. Fed up, Sada quit the business three months later.[75]

In mid-1932, when she was twenty-seven years old, she returned to Osaka's brothels. It wasn't long before Sada quit the business of prostitution again and became a mistress. During this time, she began to derive great pleasure from sex and found it difficult to sleep alone. Since her lover would only visit her five to six times a month, she took other lovers to fill the void.

Sada had three lovers simultaneously taking care of her and giving her between ¥100 and ¥160 per month to spend as she pleased. These men had been her favorite clients in the days when she had earned her living working as a prostitute.[76] One of the men was a good-looking gentleman named Yagi Kojiro. He became acquainted with Sada when she worked as a prostitute in Osaka.[77]

With no financial worries, Sada found that she had plenty of free time, which she devoted to playing mahjongg, visiting Dotonbori, and enjoying the Takarazuka Revue.[78]

Dotonbori, Osaka's lively entertainment district, owes its roots to a merchant named Doton Yasui. In 1612, he invested in an ambitious development project that entailed diverting and expanding the *Umezugawa* (Umezu River) with the hope of increasing commerce in the region. Unfortunately, the project was interrupted when he was killed during the Siege of Osaka (1614-1615). Following his death, his cousin took over the project and saw its completion in 1615. The new canal was named Dotonbori in Doton Yasui's honor.

Following the completion of the canal project, an urban development project was undertaken that brought theater companies and playhouses to the canal's south bank. At the same time, the north bank began to prosper with restaurants and teahouses catering to the theatergoers.

During the 20th century, Dotonbori was regarded as a jazz mecca littered with countless dance halls and jazz cafés catering to couples, and the male clientele and their geisha escorts.[79]

The *Takarazuka Kagekidan* (Takarazuka Revue) is an all-female musical theater troupe based in Takarazuka City, Hyogo prefecture, just 29 kilometers (18 miles) from Osaka. The women portray both the male and female roles in lavish productions based on Western style musicals, Japanese folktales, and stories adapted from *manga* (graphic novels) that particularly target the teenage female demographic.

The Revue was the brainchild of Kobayashi Ichizo and was developed as part of a strategy to lure more passengers to his trains on the Hankyu Railway system. Ichizo's original plan included only the Hankyu Department Store, which was Japan's first department store constructed inside of a train terminal, and the Takarazuka Shin-onsen hot spring resort. The resort was situated in a two-story, Western style building called Paradise. The building, which featured an indoor pool, was forced to close after only two months of operation because co-ed swimming was outlawed at the time. Furthermore, even though the Takarazuka Shin-onsen was billed as a hot spring resort, it did not have any hot spring facilities. Ichizo refused to relent and decided to use the building for entertainment purposes, thus giving rise to the Takarazuka Revue. The Revue gave its first performance on April 1, 1914, in a theater built in the converted indoor pool room. A lid placed over the pool served as the audience seating, while the changing rooms comprised the stage area.[80]

Despite her excessive spending, Sada managed to put aside ¥400, ended her relationships with her lovers, and rented an apartment in Osaka. Although she was attracted to Kojiro physically, she found it was not easy to be with him because he simply put on airs and only pretended to have money.[81] Sada also had the misfortune of being arrested for gambling, which served as the impetus for her to attempt to lead a normal life once again. She visited her parents in Saitama and remained there for three months. She might have stayed longer, had it not been for the three men from Sasayama who came to Saitama in search of her. Sada fled to Osaka once again and remained there until January of 1933, when she received a telegram informing her that her mother had passed away.[82]

One week after her mother's passing, Sada was back in Saitama. She stayed at her family's home for two weeks, but the men from the brothels were still searching for her. She departed from Saitama and traveled to Tokyo where she turned to prostitution once again. In October of 1933, she left the sex industry and became a mistress to a married businessman in his late thirties named Nakagawa Chojiro. Chojiro operated a sack business in Muromachi in the Nihonbashi ward. [83]

In January of 1934, Sada received word that her father had fallen ill. She traveled to Saitama to help nurse him back to health, but Shigeyoshi passed away ten days after her arrival, on January 26. After his passing, Sada received an inheritance of ¥300 and returned to Tokyo and her lover Chojiro.[84]

While in Tokyo, she learned that Inaba Masatake's daughter had passed away. She and Sada had been good friends, and the daughter had been instrumental in helping to re-establish the once broken working relationship between her father and Sada. Sada visited the girl's grave and purportedly gave the Inabas ¥150 after pawning one of her rings.

Things once again took a turn for the worse when Chojiro's failing health forced him to end his relationship with Sada in September of that year. Left alone, she traveled to Yokohama and found work as a prostitute at an establishment called Yamadaya. Not long afterward, she quit prostitution and became the mistress of a man named Kasahara Kinnosuke.

Kinnosuke was born in the Noge district of Yokohama's Naka ward. He was employed at the Yokohama Stock Exchange. On November 21, 1930, he was appointed as the head of the Yokohama branch of the right-wing *Rikken Seiyukai* lobbying office. The Rikken Seiyukai (Constitutional Association of

Political Friendship) was one of the main political parties in pre-World War II Japan. Founded on September 15, 1900, the party was dissolved and merged into the Imperial Rule Assistance Association on July 30, 1940.[85]

Sada met Kinnosuke in October of 1934. At the time of their meeting, he was a married man; he had been married for twenty-seven years. His wife was fifty-five years old and together they had a 20-year-old son named Kikutaro.

Kasahara Kinnosuke was an acquaintance of a man named Yamada, a brothel owner in the Naka ward. One day, the brothel was raided by the police and the prostitutes were hauled off to the Isezaki-cho Police Station. Yamada approached Kinnosuke and asked him to use his connections and influence to secure the women's release. Sada was among the women who had been arrested and confined to the police station.

Kinnosuke found Sada very attractive, and after securing her release he negotiated with Yamada to allow her to become his mistress. On December 20, he moved Sada into a house located in Miyakawa-cho. He paid her rent and gave her ¥3-¥4 every now and then for living expenses. Kinnosuke and Sada never lived together, but he visited her every other day or every two days. Gradually, his visits became less frequent.

During the course of their brief relationship, Sada suggested that he leave his wife, but he refused. As his visits declined, she asked if she could have another lover. Kinnosuke refused, and Sada fled once again. She left behind a letter telling her lover that she no longer wished to be a part of a love triangle and asked him to forget her. Kinnosuke pursued her as far as Sakaguchi, Makinohara-shi (Makinohara City) in Shizuoka, threatening her with legal action in light of the money he had wasted on her. Wanting to get as far away from him as she could, she escaped to Nagoya.

Sada welcomed the New Year in Nagoya, where she had started working at a restaurant called Kotobuki under the alias Tanaka Kayo. By April she had established a sexual liaison with one of the restaurant's customers whose name she did not know. She fabricated a story to her lover about having had a husband and infant daughter in Tokyo. She told him that her husband had passed away and she came to Nagoya in search of work.[86]

She knew that the restaurant manager would be displeased if he discovered that she was having an affair with a customer, so she quit her job at Kotobuki and started working for a small restaurant called Iju in the same neighborhood. However, by June she had already tired of Nagoya and decided to return to Tokyo. She lied to her lover once again by telling him that her daughter had passed away and she needed to return to Tokyo. Her sympathetic lover, whose name she still did not know, wished her well and gave her ¥50 to help cover her expenses. Sada took the money and departed for Tokyo, promising to write.[87]

Once back in Tokyo, Sada went to live with Inaba Masatake. Kinnosuke learned of her return to Tokyo and promptly filed a lawsuit alleging marriage fraud. With the police in pursuit, Sada left the Inaba house and started working at an unlicensed Tokyo brothel owned by an acquaintance named Kimura Hiroshi.

When the situation calmed down, she wrote to her lover in Nagoya and asked him to visit her in Tokyo. He obliged and after spending a few hours together at an inn called Yumenosato, he returned to Nagoya. Sada continued to work at the brothel and eventually became involved with the owner.

One month later, her lover from Nagoya returned to Tokyo and visited the Kimura house. Sada had lied to him by telling him that the house belonged to her sister. After talking to Hiroshi, her lover finally learned what she did for a living.[88]

The discovery did not quell his feelings for her, however, and he took her to an *onsen* (hot spring) located in the seaside resort town of Atami. While there, he told her that he would help her establish a normal life. He seemed genuinely concerned about her, but he still refused to divulge his name and profession.

When Sada returned to Tokyo, she went back to live with Masatake. She also had a series of encounters with her former lover, Nakagawa Chojiro. But not knowing the identity of her lover from Nagoya troubled her. She resolved to learn more about him and departed from Tokyo for Nagoya in August.

After stopping by an inn near the railroad station in Nagoya, she came across a newspaper headline which read, "City Council Members Go to America." The photograph corresponding to the article was that of her lover from Nagoya. For the first time, Sada learned her lover's name and profession. He was Omiya Goro.[89]

Born in the Ibaraki prefecture in 1889, Goro was a college professor, school president, and a Nagoya City Councilman with aspirations of becoming a member of the Imperial Diet.[90] The Imperial Diet was Japan's first modern legislature and had been established in 1889 by the Meiji Constitution. The Diet was comprised of a House of Representatives and a House of Peers. The House of Representatives were elected directly while the House of Peers consisted of high-ranking nobles. This changed with the adoption of the post-World War II constitution in 1947. The current legislature is known as *Kokkai* (The National Diet) and is comprised of a lower house called the House of Representatives, and an upper house, called the House of Councillors. Both houses of the Diet are directly elected.[91]

Sada telephoned Goro and they met at an inn by the harbor. He was deeply troubled by the fact that she had learned his name and profession. A year after their meeting, Sada recalled that Goro had told her that if the public were to learn of his relationship with a prostitute, his life as a school president would be ruined. He asked her to keep things quiet until after he became a Diet member.

On August 13, 1935, Goro and Sada met again in Tokyo as he was about to depart for America. Goro departed from Yokohama aboard the *Heian Maru* and arrived in Vancouver on August 26.[92] He returned to Japan in October and Sada was once again united with her lover in mid-November. She was suffering from the symptoms of syphilis at the time so he gave her ¥250 and sent her to a hot spring resort in Kusatsu. It was a common belief at the time that onsen waters would cure syphilis. Sada remained at the resort through January, 1936. During that time, Goro visited her only once.

Shortly after her return to Tokyo from Kusatsu, Sada met Goro in Kyoto. During this meeting, he made a suggestion that she start a business—perhaps open up an oden shop (oden is a Japanese winter one-pot dish typically consisting of fish cakes, hard-boiled eggs, and daikon radish as the main ingredients) or a small restaurant. Sada had seen other women successfully managing restaurants and was aware of the financial freedom it afforded them. Determined, she set out to find a job that would provide her with the necessary skills and knowledge to run a restaurant.[93]

CHAPTER V

Sada and Kichi Together

"He was the first man I had ever met who made a woman feel important and who would do things to make her happy, and I fell completely in love with him."

-Abe Sada (Interrogation, 1936)[94]

IN FEBRUARY OF 1936, through the introduction of an acquaintance, Sada accepted a position as a maid at a restaurant called Yoshidaya located in Tokyo's Nakano ward. The Nakano ward had only been in existence since October 1, 1932, when the towns of Nogata and Nakano were absorbed into Tokyo City and a special ward was created. The restaurant, which specialized in eel dishes, was opened in 1920 by the then twenty-six-year-old Ishida Kichizo. Now, at the age of forty-two, Kichizo primarily spent his days womanizing and the restaurant was actually run by his wife. The couple had two teenage children, a son and a daughter.[95]

There were a total of five maids at that time who worked and lived at Yoshidaya. When Sada, who had adopted the alias Okayo, first interviewed at the restaurant, both Kichizo and his wife had asked her why she wanted to work there. She fabricated a story about her husband's business going bankrupt and requiring her to work; therefore, Kichizo was operating under the knowledge that Sada was a married woman. The knowledge did not prevent him from sexually pursuing her, however. Within ten days after becoming employed at Yoshidaya, Kichizo resorted to blocking her passage in narrow hallways, standing uncomfortably close to her, and staring at her. As time passed, he became more physical, hugging and kissing her whenever he had the chance.

Sada had become a maid at Yoshidaya with the hope that she would be able to learn the secret of Kichizo's success and apply that knowledge to open her own business. However, she eventually ended up giving in to the playboy's advances while she continued to see her lover, Goro, on the side.

She often thought about Goro and wanted to be with him; however, he was not the kind of man who would nurture her impulses. When she asked him to write her letters while they were apart, he refused and merely told her that even if they were separated for five years or ten years, he would not forget her. Although Sada realized that she needed to be patient with Goro, his unwillingness to satisfy her needs made it easy for her to have an affair with someone else.[96]

One particular evening, Sada was asked by Kichizo's wife to serve sake to a customer waiting in the restaurant's annex. When Sada arrived with the sake, she was surprised to see that the customer was none other than Kichizo. He liked to drink at home and was in the habit of hiring geishas to entertain him while he drank. On that night, employer and employee became lovers, and Sada soon developed an infatuation for Kichizo. From that point on, whenever they could sneak away, they would go to the annex on the second floor of Yoshidaya and engage in sex.

On April 19, Yoshidaya was hosting a large party and everyone at the restaurant was busy working. Taking advantage of the situation, Sada and Kichizo stole away to the parlor, turned off the lights, and proceeded to make love. A maid unexpectedly came in to pick up a *zabuton* (floor cushion) and discovered them. When Sada and Kichizo's secret was revealed, Kichizo's wife became extremely angry, severely chiding him in the process. However, since she had run away with a man just a few years earlier and Kichizo had taken her back, she was not in a position to argue too adamantly about the incident.

She did, however, take every opportunity to warn the other maids about her husband's womanizing. When Sada stayed by her bedside for two or three days nursing her back to health after she had taken ill, she learned that Kichizo had kept a mistress for six years. But Sada was not stirred by the wife's stories. She knew that their marriage was a charade and justified having an affair with Kichizo on that basis.

Kichizo told Sada that he did not love his wife and he had only taken her back for the sake of their children. He was a man who believed that no matter how often a man cheated on his wife, a wife cheating on her husband was unforgiveable.

Not wanting to risk getting caught again, Sada and Kichizo made plans to meet outside of Yoshidaya. On April 23, they met at an *ochaya* (tea house) in Shibuya called Mitsuwa for what was supposed to be a quick tryst, but it ended up becoming a two-week long lovemaking marathon.[97] In those days, an ochaya was equivalent to the modern-day love hotel in Japan. Private tea houses with private rooms catering to prostitutes and their clients had existed in Japan since the Tokugawa era.[98]

It was during this meeting that Sada learned the truth about Yoshidaya. Kichizo informed Sada that the restaurant's finances were poor and she would not be able to work there for too much longer. He told her that she should try to start a business, perhaps run a small inn, which would enable them to carry on their affair much longer. Kichizo's confession about Yoshidaya's financial troubles conveyed his intimacy toward her; or at least that is what Sada thought since she knew that he had not shared the information with his wife.

Sada and Kichizo spent April 23 through the 27 at Mitsuwa where they remained in bed the entire time. They did not bother to disengage even when the maids entered their room to serve tea and sake.[99]

When they became concerned about the possibility of Kichizo's wife calling Mitsuwa, they moved to another teahouse called Tagawa in Futako Tamagawa in the Setagaya ward. They remained there from the evening of April 27 until the morning of April 29, making love as they had done at Mitsuwa. Sada and Kichizo were so infatuated with one another that they did not want to part ways, but they were running out of money. In addition to paying for the rooms at the teahouses, they were spending money on drinking and hiring geishas to entertain them. Sada did not want Kichizo to return to his wife and decided that she would go see Goro to ask him for money.

On April 29, after borrowing ¥10 from a friend in Asakusa, she departed Tokyo for Nagoya. She met Goro on April 30, but they did not sleep together. Instead, they talked for approximately an hour and a half, and Sada fabricated another lie to justify asking for money. She asked for ¥200, but Goro only had ¥100 with him at the time. He promised her that he would give her the rest when he visited her in Tokyo five days later.

Sada was unable to get Kichizo off of her mind and sent him a letter while she was away in Nagoya. She was madly obsessed with Kichizo, but because Goro had shown genuine concern for her future and well-being, she was unwilling to give up on him entirely.

After departing from Goro, she rushed back to Tokyo and met Kichizo at Kanda Station. The lovers returned to Tagawa, but the owner wanted to settle their bill, so they left without paying. They checked in to another ochaya located on Ogu-cho called Masaki, where they remained until May 1. Ogu-cho was situated within a flourishing red-light district. The Masaki ochaya was used primarily by prostitutes and their clients.[100]

Late in the evening on May 1, Sada and Kichizo departed for Tagawa with the intent of paying their bill, and stayed there until the evening of May 3. Tagawa was owned by a former geisha who was well acquainted with both Kichizo and his business, Yoshidaya. Sada and Kichizo were concerned that she might call the restaurant wanting to discuss money with Kichizo's wife, so they paid part of what they owed and left.

They told the owner that they would return on the sixth of May to settle the remainder of their bill.

Although they only had ¥20 remaining, they were unwilling to say their farewells just yet. Since Sada was planning to meet Goro on May 5 to get more money, they decided to travel back to Masaki, hire a geisha, and stay in bed the entire time until the fifth of May arrived.

On May 5, Sada was supposed to meet Goro at noon in Shinjuku, but she was running late because she had been in bed with Kichizo. Goro had waited for her and when she did not arrive as planned, he decided to sit down and have a meal. When Sada finally arrived, he was a little drunk. He told her that he would give her ¥1,000 to either help her start a business or quit seeing him altogether. Sada protested and told him that she did not want to stop seeing him. They didn't have sex that night, but he gave her ¥120 and they promised to meet again on May 15. Sada felt sorry for Goro, but she hurried back to Kichizo.

She returned to Masaki at 10:00 PM and found Kichizo in bed waiting for her. After being apart for only two or three hours, they celebrated their reunion by making love. Sada forgot about Goro completely.

Afterwards, they telephoned Inaba Masatake who told them that his phone had been ringing off the hook with Kichizo's wife calling. Sada and Kichizo knew that they were going to suffer for their indiscretion and decided that they were just going to enjoy themselves for the time being.

On the evening of May 6 it was drizzling outside, and Sada was very upset that she and Kichizo had to separate for a while. When she thought about him returning to his wife, she began to cry—and Kichizo cried also. They departed from Masaki and walked around for some time before hiring a taxi to take them to Asakusa. After they arrived in Asakusa, they walked around in the park and went to a nearby restaurant to have drinks. They remained there, talking and drinking, until closing time at midnight. The more time they spent together, the more difficult it became to part ways. They continued to walk together and visited a sweets shop along the way. From there they went to another restaurant where they drank until its closing time at 2:00 AM. They left that restaurant and walked around a little more in Yanagibashi. At around 3:00 AM, they finally turned to walk toward Kichizo's house. Still unwilling to separate, they found a place in Shinjuku where they drank beer until 4:00 AM. They made love one final time, and at 9:00 AM on May 7, Sada departed for Masatake's house and Kichizo went home to his wife.[101]

By now, Sada had become completely obsessed with Kichizo and grew exceedingly jealous as she thought about him returning to his wife. To calm herself, she smoked and drank heavily while she was at Masatake's place.

In recounting the days she spent apart from Kichizo, Sada claimed that she had fallen madly in love with him and felt incomplete without him. She convinced herself that the next time they saw one another, she would do whatever it took to keep him from going back to his wife.[102]

One day, she went to see a play to distract herself from her thoughts of Kichizo. The story featured a geisha who killed her lover with a knife to prevent him from leaving her. In the 1930s, topics such as these were not uncommon in Japanese theater. In fact, the filmmaker, screenwriter, and producer, Naruse Mikio, dominated Japanese cinema at the time with films that were imbued with pointlessness and often featured a female protagonist (a geisha).[103] Deeply affected by the play, Sada visited the Kikuhide Cutlery Store the next day and purchased a large kitchen knife.

When Sada and Kichizo had parted in Shinjuku on May 7, they had talked about getting back together in five or six days. However, Sada was so obsessed that she could not wait. She placed a call to the Tama Sushi restaurant where they said that they would exchange calls and messages so that Kichizo's wife would not become suspicious. When they spoke on the phone, Kichizo once again reiterated that they should wait until May 14, but Sada was so drunk and desperate that she told him that she could not wait.

On May 11, Sada and Kichizo met at Nakano Station. Sada was so elated to see him that in her rush to get out of the taxi she almost fell to the ground. When she saw that he was wearing a nice kimono she became jealous. Without hesitation, she pulled out the kitchen knife that she had purchased and half-jokingly threatened him with it. She accused him of wearing the kimono to please his favorite customer and she vowed that she would kill him for doing so. Sada's actions startled Kichizo initially and he drew back a little, but he laughed and seemed delighted afterwards. Amidst his laughter, he advised her to put away the knife before they got themselves into real trouble.[104]

After enjoying drinks at an oden shop near the station, they traveled to Masaki. Kichizo told Sada that he had not slept with his wife while they were apart, but Sada was so jealous that she did not believe him. She pinched, hit, and bit him out of jealousy, but Kichizo did not get angry. He asked her to forgive him, and as she continued to playfully torture him, he asked her not to kill him. Despite her irrepressible jealousy, Sada was elated to see Kichizo again. She later recalled that she felt as though she was seeing the man of her dreams for the first time after being away from him for 100 years.[105] For Kichizo, on the other hand, it was a journey that would prove to be deadly.[106]

Sada and Kichizo remained together until May 13. From early evening on the 13th until 11:00 AM on the 15th, Sada was with Goro. She met him at Tokyo Station, and after having lunch at Ginza they rented a room at Yumenosato, where they spent the night together. This time, she had sex with him out of obligation and thought about Kichizo the entire time. Before they parted, he gave her ¥50.[107]

When Sada returned to Masaki, Kichizo teased her about being with another man and joked that he would go out and buy a big knife the next time. They began to make love and experimented with various erotic acts including asphyxiation, using the sash from Sada's kimono. Kichizo told Sada that he had heard how asphyxia increased sexual pleasure.[108]

On the 16th, Sada gave Kichizo money to get his hair cut. While he was away, she asked a maid to deliver a letter to Goro, who was staying at the Manseikan in Kanda. After Kichizo returned, they resumed their lovemaking. They had continuous sex through the 18th.

On that day, they made love for two hours, with Sada choking Kichizo on and off during sex. At one point, Sada pulled the sash chord too tight and Kichizo raised up off of the futon and wrapped his arms around her; he appeared to be crying. He told her that his face felt as if it were on fire. Sada soon realized that his face was rather red and his eyes were swollen. There was a mark around his neck where the sash had been. She washed his face, put him to bed, and continued to wipe his face to cool his skin until morning came. When Kichizo woke up, he saw his face in the mirror and jokingly chided Sada for being cruel.[109]

When Kichizo's face did not return to normal, they considered calling a doctor, but feared that a doctor may alert the police. Instead, Sada left to consult with a pharmacist and to pick up some medicine. Kichizo was afraid to go out looking as he did and remained in the room the entire time.

The prognosis Sada received from the pharmacist was not a good one. He told her that the blood vessels were swollen and there was nothing that could be done. He advised her to let the injured person rest quietly. He also mentioned that it might take a month or two for injured face to return to normal.

In order to aid Kichizo's red, swollen eyes, Sada purchased powdered eye medicine and left the pharmacy to have dinner. She returned to the pharmacy afterwards and while she was waiting for the eye medicine to be prepared, the pharmacist told her about a medication called Calmotin that could help Kichizo relax.[110] Calmotin is one of the names of the hypnotic and sedative compound Bromisoval marketed over the counter in Asia. It was discovered by the German pharmaceutical company, Knoll Pharmaceuticals, in 1907.[111] The pharmacist prescribed the medication for Kichizo with a strict warning that he was not to take more than three tablets at a time.

When Kichizo learned the outcome, he grew despondent. Despite the pharmacist's warning, he swallowed five to six caplets of Calmotin after dinner, telling Sada that three would not suffice.

Also, Kichizo wanted to leave the ochaya as soon as possible because they did not have enough money to sustain them. This displeased Sada immensely. In trying to appease her, Kichizo suggested that they go to a friend's house and stay there. Sada rejected that suggestion, frustrating Kichizo. He finally told her that she knew from the beginning that he had children and they could not stay together forever. After hearing this, Sada assumed that Kichizo was trying to leave her and began to cry. Upon seeing her reaction, Kichizo became teary-eyed and tried his best to comfort her. Sada did not hear what he was saying and the only thing she could focus on was what they needed to do to stay together.

While they were in this state, the maid brought the soup they had ordered to their room. Kichizo ingested the remaining twelve to thirteen tablets of Calmotin with his soup. They went to bed at midnight, and after having sex, Kichizo fell asleep.[112]

As Kichizo slept, Sada lay awake thinking about her future with the man she loved. She knew it was out of the question for Kichizo to leave his wife as that would entail abandoning his children. She also knew that he would never agree to a double-suicide for the same reason. She became increasingly tormented knowing that she could not bear to be without him.

She believed that if they parted this time, it would be several months before they were reunited. She was worried that Kichizo would embrace his wife again and she did not want to let him leave. While Kichizo slept, he opened his eyes from time to time to see if Sada was still beside him. After seeing that she was, he would go back to sleep.

At one point, during one of these waking moments, he told Sada that he thought she would strangle him while he was sleeping; she told him that she would. He continued by telling her not to stop if she did, because the pain afterwards was unbearable.

In the early hours of May 18, as Kichizo slept, Sada wrapped her peach kimono sash around his neck twice and began to asphyxiate him. He opened his eyes and uttered her name, "Okayo," as his body raised up and moved as if he was going to hug her. Sada placed her face against his chest and she asked him to forgive her. With that, she pulled the sash with all of her might. Kichizo moaned and his hands shook violently, but Sada continued to apply pressure. Once his body had gone limp, Sada released the ends of the sash.

Trembling, she finished off the sake that had been brought to their room earlier. She moved back over to where Kichizo was laying and decided to make sure that he would not be revived. She knotted the sash across his throat, wrapped the rest around his neck, and placed the ends under his pillow. She went downstairs to see if anyone was around and saw that the clock on the desk indicated that it was 2:00 AM.

In her testimony, Sada said that she felt completely at ease after killing Kichizo. She claimed that she sensed that a heavy burden had been lifted from her shoulders and she gained a sense of clarity.[113]

After returning to the room, she laid next to Kichizo's lifeless body for a few hours before emasculating him with the kitchen knife. She initially placed the severed genitalia in a tissue, but saw that blood was pouring out of Kichizo's wound. She removed the severed body parts from the tissue and placed the tissue over his wound to absorb the blood. She dipped her finger in his blood and wrote, *Sada Kichi futari kiri* (Sada Kichi only two of us) on Kichizo's left thigh and on the bedding. With the kitchen knife she carved her name, *Sada*, on his left arm.

She later ripped the cover off the magazine that was next to Kichizo's pillow and wrapped his severed genitalia in it. She tried to clean up the room before she left and ended up dropping the lid of the wash basin in the toilet.

Next, she put on Kichizo's *nagajuban* (under kimono) and underwear, placed his severed genitalia (still wrapped in the magazine cover) next to her stomach, and wrapped the kitchen knife to take it with her. She kissed Kichizo goodbye and covered his body with the *kakefuton* (Japanese comforter). She departed the ochaya at approximately 8:00 AM and made her escape in a taxi.[114]

Before leaving, she remembered that she had sent a letter to Goro on May 16 and realized that the police might investigate him once the murder was discovered. She decided to go see him and apologize.

They met in front of Manso in Kanda-Sudacho (a district in Tokyo) and went to a noodle shop in Nihonbashi for lunch. During lunch, Goro told Sada that he had resigned as the school president. From there they rented a room at Midoriya, where they made love for a few hours. Sada apologized to Goro over and over again. He, of course, was unaware of the murder and assumed that she was apologizing to him for having taken another lover. In fact, Sada's apologies were for the damage she knew she was about to cause to his political career. Although Goro suggested that they meet again on May 25, Sada never saw him again.[115]

Before departing Masaki, Sada had told the staff that she was going out to purchase confections and asked that they not disturb Kichizo as he was still sleeping. When Sada did not return by 2:30 in the afternoon, a maid entered the room and discovered Kichizo's dead body.[116]

When later questioned about why she had mutilated Kichizo's body, Sada responded that she had cut off his genitalia because she did not want his wife to touch them while she was washing his dead body. She said that she had written, *Sada Kichi only two of us,* because she wanted to imply that he belonged to her and her only. She had carved her name on his arm because she wanted to become a part of him. She had put on his underwear and nagajuban because they had his smell and it made her feel as though she was still with him.[117]

CHAPTER VI

Go Ichi-Hachi Jiken

"Just as when men redeem a geisha so that they can keep her all to themselves, there are women who are so enraptured with a man that they think of doing what I did. They just don't act it out."

Abe Sada (Interrogation, 1936)[118]

THE DAY AFTER the murder, Sada's actions were quite out of the ordinary for someone who had just taken another person's life. On May 19, she went shopping and saw a film. On May 20, she checked into an inn located in the Shinagawa district. [119] During the Tokugawa period, Shinagawa was a *shukuba* (post town) catering to travelers setting out on the Tokaido Highway from Edo to Kyoto. As a result, the Shinagawa district was, and continues to be, home to many hotels and inns.[120]

Newspapers described a sexually and criminally dangerous woman on the loose triggering an Abe Sada panic. Following the murder, numerous mistaken sightings of Sada occurred around the country. One suspected sighting in a Tokyo shopping district caused a massive stampede.[121]

Ishida Kichizo's death caused a national sensation. The crime was satirically dubbed the *Go Ichi-Hachi Jiken* (the May

18 Incident) in reference to a failed coup d'état attempt known as the *Ni Ni-Roku Jiken* (the February 26 Incident), which had taken place in Tokyo earlier that year.

The Ni Ni-Roku Jiken was staged by young military officers belonging to the Imperial Way Faction. The insurrectionists seemingly acted in Emperor Hirohito's name and hoped to spark a general uprising. However, the Emperor was not on their side and he acted decisively to suppress the coup.

The army, at that time, was divided into two factions, the Imperial Way Faction and the Control Faction. The first group valued spiritual purity and advocated attacking the Soviet Union. The second group was dominated by top military staff and supported centralized economic and military planning, technological modernization, and expansionism in China.[122]

The Imperial Way Faction was angered by the success of the liberals in the parliamentary elections that had been held a week before the attempted coup.[123] The young officers believed that the problems facing the nation were the result of Japan straying away from the essence of *kokutai* (the system of government involving the proper relationship between the Emperor, the people, and the state). They called themselves the "Righteous Army" and adopted the slogan "Revere the Emperor, Destroy the Traitors." By leading a general uprising, they hoped to instigate a "Showa Restoration" (named after the Meiji Restoration of 1868) that would enable the Emperor to reclaim his authority and purge Japan of Western ideas and those who exploited the people.[124]

With 1,400 soldiers on their side, the insurgents utilized the Sanno Hotel in Akasaka as their command post. Their plan was to occupy the prime minister's residence, the Metropolitan Police Headquarters, and other buildings. One of their prime targets was Finance Minister Takahashi Korekiyo, who advocated reduced military spending to promote fiscal consolidation. A lieutenant in the Righteous Army led a contingent of 120 men to the finance minister's residence in Aoyama and killed Korekiyo while he was asleep. The Lord Keeper of the Privy Seal, Saito Makoto, and the Inspector

General of Military Education, Watanabe Jotaro, and approximately half a dozen civilian police officers were also killed. The Prime Minister, Okada Keisuke, escaped death by hiding in a closet, but his brother-in-law, Matsuo Denzo, was mistakenly killed instead.[26]

By the order of the Emperor, the rebels were arrested and Martial Law was declared for three days. Order was restored in Tokyo by February 29, 1936.

Those who had participated in the coup were court martialed. A secret trial followed during which the defendants had no legal representation and could not call witnesses or appeal the verdict. When it was all over, nineteen of the coup leaders were executed for mutiny and another forty were imprisoned.[125]

Sada saw one of the evening newspapers in which she was compared to Takahashi Oden.[126] Takahashi Oden (1848-1879) gained notoriety after she was found guilty of ruthlessly slitting her lover's throat and leaving him in a pool of his own blood. She was also suspected of poisoning her husband. Oden was sentenced to death and was the last woman in Japan to die by beheading. It is said that it took several blows to execute her because she fiercely kicked and screamed in resistance.

After the execution, her body was taken to a hospital affiliated with the *Keishicho* (Tokyo Metropolitan Police) and dissected by an army surgeon named Osanai Ken and three other doctors. The surgeons focused primarily on Oden's genitalia in an effort to observe any abnormalities, which might have accounted for her behavior. At the time, a new field of study known as *zokakiron* (anatomical studies of genital organs) was emerging. After the autopsy was completed, Osanai issued a report citing "Abnormal thickness and swelling of the labia minor. Over-development of clitoris. Enlargement of vagina." It was his opinion that these physical abnormalities were the cause of her violent nature.[127]

At the inn in Shinagawa, Sada drank heavily and ordered a masseuse to come to her room. She wrote letters to Goro and Kurokawa Hana, Inaba Masatake's wife. She also penned an emotional message to her deceased lover, Kichizo. During her interrogation, she said that she had intended to commit suicide by jumping off of Mount Ikoma, located on the border of Nara and Osaka prefectures. The letters she had written expressed her gratitude and hinted that she intended to depart this world. Her letter to Kichizo said, "You died and became mine. I will come soon."[128]

Had it not been for the fact that police were posted at all of the train stations in and around Tokyo, Yokohama, and Osaka, Sada would have reached Mount Ikoma. She had purchased a train ticket to Osaka, which she asked the innkeeper to get refunded when she realized that she could not travel by train. She thought about hanging herself at the inn, but the distance between the ceiling and the floor was not adequate and her feet touched the ground. She resigned herself to being arrested and changed rooms at the inn.

After Kichizo's body was discovered, the Tokyo police launched a citywide dragnet for Sada.[129] A detective known as Ando Matsukichi arrived at the inn where Sada was staying at approximately 4:00 PM on May 20. He asked to review the inn's register. One name on the register caught his attention; it was the name Owada Nao. Nao is a common feminine Japanese given name which is occasionally used by males. Matsukichi asked to be taken to the room where Owada Nao was staying and the hotel staff obliged. Upon entering the room he was calmly greeted by Sada, who was dressed in a sleeping gown. She had stayed up until 1:00 AM waiting for the police to come through her door. She got up without hesitation, got dressed, and put on her makeup. She was escorted out of the inn by the police around 5:30 PM.[130]

Following the arrest, detective Ando Matsukichi received a commendation from the Tokyo Metropolitan Police.[131]

Insurgents occupying the Sanno Hotel during Ni Ni-Roku Jiken in
February 1936

A Mainichi Newspaper article about the Abe Sada Incident featuring a photo of
Ishida Kichizo. The headline reads, "Mature beauty with yakaimaki hairstyle
murdered her husband out of jouchi (losing control from lust/love). Wrote with
dripping blood SADA AND KICHI TOGETHER. Disappeared in entaku (taxi)."

May 20, 1936 photo of Abe Sada leaving the Takanawa Police Station in Tokyo

CHAPTER VII

Captured

"Nothing has been so painful in all my life as the time between the eighth and the tenth, when I felt incredibly jealous and irritable."

Abe Sada (Interrogation, 1936)[132]

FOLLOWING HER ARREST on the afternoon of May 20, Sada was taken to the Takanawa Police Station, located approximately 5.79 km (3.60 miles) from Shinagawa. Her interrogation lasted over a month and was broken up into eight separate sessions. Certain facts from her interrogation were leaked to the press and caused the public's fascination with Sada to intensify, turning her into an overnight celebrity.[133]

She was confined in the Ichigaya Prison located in the eastern portion of Shinjuku, Tokyo. During her first night of confinement, a guard reported hearing her repeatedly say in a faint voice, "My heart hurts, my heart hurts." When she returned to her cell after her first interrogation session, she reportedly told the guard in a sad voice, "I am going to die." When the guard told her that she would not be given the death penalty, Sada responded by saying that it would be better if she were sentenced to die.[134]

Sada provided the investigators with an extremely detailed confession, which was later published and quickly became a national bestseller.[135] She willingly cooperated with the police and provided as much detail as she could in order to convey to the police and to the court that she was neither mentally, criminally, nor sexually deranged. Her interrogating officer, Adachi Umezo, confirmed this in the police investigation record by stating, "She answered questions without hesitation and she didn't wring her hands. The interrogation was easy. She said I'm very sorry for all the trouble I've caused with great fervor, but it was possible to see that deep inside she was very satisfied that she had managed to take complete control of the man she loved. I could tell that when I was sitting across from her.... Nevertheless, there was nothing about her that made her seem criminal."[136]

Sada's trial began on November 25, 1936, and crowds gathered outside the Tokyo District Court at 5:00 AM to catch a glimpse of her. Inside, the courtroom was packed with 200 spectators, the majority of whom were young women.[137] Sada arrived at and departed from the courthouse through an underground passageway. She wore a strange conical hat woven from straw to hide her face. Her left hand was bandaged, and in her right hand she clutched a white handkerchief.[138]

Prior to 2006, court-appointed attorneys were assigned to defendants only after an indictment.[139] Sada was aided by two attorneys, Oku Kinjiro and Takeuchi Kintaro, both of whom she fired on October 9. Sada claimed that she would not object to the court's decision, regardless of what it may be. For this reason, she decided that she did not need to be represented by a lawyer. However, she feared that she would be misunderstood and portrayed as a lunatic and decided to re-hire Takeuchi Kintaro to argue her case in court.[140]

Although Japan introduced trial by jury in 1923, it was seldom used after it went into effect in 1928. Therefore, Sada's case was not heard by a jury but by three judges charged with passing down their sentences once all of the evidence had been presented.[141] In Japan, if the lawful punishment for a crime is not severe, a single judge may preside over the trial. Otherwise, a three-judge panel is generally required.[142] The lead judge of the three-judge panel was 43-year old Hosoya Keijiro (b. 1893).

Keijiro was an interesting choice for the judge to preside over Sada's case. Although he was a married man, he was known to frequent hostess cafés regularly. Hostess cafés in Japan generally employ women who use *genji-na* (professional names). These women entertain their customers by lighting their cigarettes, pouring their beverages, and offering flirtatious conversation. Sada previously worked as a café hostess and it is safe to assume that the judge was well acquainted with women of her background.

Before 1868, a unified criminal justice system did not exist in Japan. The code of conduct was determined by Confucian ideals, and those who failed to adhere to these ideals were judged and punished by public officials representing their specific domains. Enforcement varied from one domain to another, but justice was generally harsh and its severity depended upon the offender's status. The offender's family and neighbors were often forced to share the guilt.

After the Meiji Restoration of 1868, Japan adopted a legal system modeled after the French legal framework known as the Napoleonic Code. The Japanese Penal Code and the Code of Criminal Instruction were both enacted in 1880. Offenses and penalties were specifically outlined, a centralized administration of criminal justice was established, and all citizens were treated as equals. Also, collective guilt and guilt by association were abolished. In 1907, the Penal Code was revised to reflect the growing influence of German law in Japan. [143] Germany uses an inquisitorial system where the judges are actively involved in investigating the facts of the case, as opposed to an adversarial system where the role of the judge is that of an impartial mediator between the prosecutor or plaintiff and the defendant.[144]

In Sada's case, the structure of the evidence presented in court was primarily determined by the police. The evidence was presented in three bound volumes and included the notes from her interrogation as well as the police investigation record.[145]

The police investigation included a statement by an expert witness, Matsumura Tsuneo. Tsuneo was a physician and lecturer at Tokyo University who had been tasked with examining Sada both physically and psychologically. Fifty-seven years earlier, a post-mortem dissection was conducted on Takahashi Oden to determine if physical abnormalities contributed to her deranged, criminal behavior. During Sada's trial, it was clear that the Japanese still believed that physical abnormalities contributed to the deranged behavior of criminals.

After concluding his examination, Tsuneo made the following statement. "It is not possible to diagnose any mental abnormality at the time the defendant committed the murder."[146]

The mass media relayed as much of Sada's sensational testimony as government censors would allow, thus fueling the public's growing fascination with her. One leading newspaper described the public's enthrallment as "Sada mania." The young women who followed the case were called "Sada fans." [147] The public frenzy was not just about Sada, however. The media also reported on the police investigation of Sada's former lover, Omiya Goro, for his possible involvement in the murder. Although he was found innocent, he was forced to resign from his political post and eventually disappeared from public view altogether. Kichizo's widow was seemingly devastated by her husband's death, even though she was well aware of his philandering. Due to the publicity of the crime, the Yoshidaya restaurant flourished as did the inn where the murder had taken place. Many couples who booked reservations at the inn specifically requested the room where Kichizo was murdered.[148]

The trial itself was relatively short as Sada simply pleaded guilty to the charges brought against her. Nonetheless, as a matter of protocol, the court called numerous witnesses, including Sada's sister, and Kichizo's severed genitals were presented as evidence. The witness testimonies did little to sway the judges' decision. The verdict was clear from the beginning; the only thing that remained was for the judges to reach an agreement on the sentence that was to be imposed.

The sentencing hearing took place on December 8. Sada requested the death penalty so that she could be united with Kichizo. The prosecution sought imprisonment for ten years. In the end, the court found her guilty of second degree murder and the mutilation of a corpse. During her interrogation, Sada had also admitted to having engaged in an act of necrophilia with Kichizo's severed body parts.

On December 21, the court handed down a sentence of only six years, which would include the seven months she had already served.[149] The lead judge explained their decision by stressing the role the victim played in the events that led to his death. He declared, "The victim in this crime was himself lascivious and old enough to understand the consequences of his actions. In this way, it is impossible to overlook how [the victim] was central in causing this crime."[150] He also focused on Sada's mental state at the time.

Sada had been assessed by both Kaneko Junji, the police psychologist, and Matsumura Tsuneo, the court-appointed expert witness.

Junji's opinion that Sada was afflicted with sadism, masochism, fetishism, and nymphomania, and that she had chosen prostitution by her free will, was readily picked up by the newspapers reporting the trial.[151] He failed to mention anything about the fact that she had been raped at age fifteen and was sold into prostitution by her father in the years that followed. He neglected to include any mention of her attempts to run away from prostitution only to be chased down, captured, brought back, and sent to another brothel far worse than the one from which she had tried to escape.

Matsumura Tsuneo made a similar assessment, stating that Sada exhibited hysteria, nymphomania, sadism, fetishism, and alcohol use.[152]

Further, and despite her objections, Sada's attorney, Takeuchi Kintaro, also pleaded that she had been insane at the time of the murder. The judge concluded that the six-year sentence was sufficient time for Sada to rehabilitate herself in prison and start a new life upon her release.[153]

Sada had been confined to Ichigaya Prison since her arrest.[154] This was the same prison where the Korean independence activist, Lee Bong-chang, was executed in 1932. On January 9, 1932, Lee Bong-chang had attempted to assassinate Emperor Hirohito as he was departing from the Imperial Palace via the Sakuradamon Gate to view a military parade. Lee approached the Emperor's carriage disguised as a Kempeitai military policeman and threw a hand grenade toward the carriage. Fortunately for the Emperor, the hand grenade missed its target and exploded near the carriage of the Imperial Household Minister, Baron Kitokuro Ichiki, instead. Lee Bong-chang was quickly apprehended by the Imperial Guard and the incident became known as The Sakuradamon Incident.[155]

Ichigaya Prison was not just any prison, and it had a long history. It owed its roots to *Denma-cho Royashiki* (Denma-cho Prison). The facility had served as a prison and execution grounds from 1613 to 1875. Located near Nihonbashi, on the outskirts of town, it was the largest prison in Edo (Tokyo) at the time. It is estimated that between 100,000 and 200,000 people had been executed at Denma-cho during the prison's two hundred and sixty-two year history. While the prison had a section for commoners, it was primarily used to incarcerate high-ranking officials. The prison's female inmates were housed in a section called the *ageya*.[156]

On December 26, Sada was transferred to Tochigi Women's Prison, located approximately 60 miles north of Tokyo, where she served out her sentence. She was confined in Cell Block 1 in a stark, three straw mat cell (the Japanese refer to the size of a room by the number of *tatami* (straw) mats that fit inside it. A tatami measures three feet by six feet), and referred to as prisoner number eleven.[157]

Kichizo's severed genitalia, which had been presented in court as evidence, were later put on display in the Tokyo University Medical School Pathology Museum as his family did not come forward to claim them. After WWII the preserved body parts mysteriously disappeared and were never seen again.[158]

As the judge had predicted, Sada's time in prison became the most stable period of her life. She later described the prison staff as "loving and caring people," and actually felt that she was a part of a community. She did face several setbacks, however, especially on the first anniversary of Kichizo's death; but she was able to function and even managed to study Nichiren Buddhist philosophy while confined.[159]

Sada became a model prisoner and her sentence was commuted in 1940 as part of a general amnesty issued by the Emperor to commemorate the 2,600[th] anniversary of the founding of the Japanese empire.[160]

The Kojiki, the oldest existing chronicle in Japan, which dates from the early eighth century, and the Nihon Shoki, the second-oldest book of classical Japanese history, both state that the first Emperor of Japan, Emperor Jimmu, ascended the throne in 660 BC. Although the stories of accession were entirely mythical, the government of Japan under the Meiji Constitution of 1889 accepted the event as historical. Therefore, 1940 was designated as the 2,600[th] anniversary of the founding of Japan.

National Foundation festivals and celebrations were held annually in Japan starting in 1872; however, the event in 1940 was the grandest to date. Initially, the Summer Olympics were slated to be hosted in Japan in 1940 and, at the same time, a lavish Tokyo Exposition was to take place. But, due to Japan's escalating war in China and the beginning of war in Europe in 1939, the Olympic Games were moved to Helsinki, Finland and the Exposition was cancelled. As a result, the Japanese redirected their efforts to commemorating the 2,600[th] anniversary of the founding of Japan by the mythical Emperor Jimmu. [161]

The practice of offering amnesty to convicted criminals has long been a tradition carried out by the Emperor during festive occasions such as a coronation. Japanese law defines five levels of pardons: amnesty, special amnesty, commutation of sentence (usually by one degree), exoneration, and the full restoration of the criminal's rights. These are determined according to the recommendations of a penal review board. [162]

A parade celebrating 2,600 years of the Japanese Empire. This photo was taken in front of the Taihoku Public Hall.

Abe Sada attends script reading

CHAPTER VIII

Aftermath

*"When I arrived at the prison and saw Ishida in my dreams I still
adored him and felt happy, but little by little my feelings
changed....and now I think it would have been better not to have
done that. I regret having done something so very stupid."*

Abe Sada (Interrogation, 1936)[163]

SADA WAS RELEASED from prison on May 17, 1941, almost
five years after the murder. Authorities aided her in registering
under a new identity, Yoshii Masako, the name she had
previously used while she was working as a café hostess. With
no income of her own, she went to live with her sister and
brother-in-law until wartime rationing required her to find a job
to support herself. Sada managed to find work as a maid, but she
was dismissed from her job when her employers discovered her
true identity.[164]

Japan's involvement in war made it very difficult for single
women to find work during this time, especially for those with
Sada's education and skill level. Forced to survive, she once
again became a mistress. She never divulged the man's name to
the public and simply referred to him in her memoirs as "Y."
Her lover knew her true identity, but he faithfully kept her
secret.[165] Sada described this period in her life as a difficult one

because she was troubled by her feelings that she was betraying Kichizo.

In late 1943, the United States Air Force intensified its air raids over Japan, forcing the Japanese government to implement plans to evacuate non-essential personnel from Tokyo, Nagoya, Osaka, and the cities in northern Kyushu. The evacuations were formally initiated on October 15, 1943. Sada and her lover were among the approximately 8.5 million civilians displaced from their homes between 1943 and 1945.[166] They spent the war years in Ibaraki and returned to Tokyo only briefly after the war ended. Y's family circumstances demanded that they relocate to yet another rural location, and they settled in the Saitama prefecture.[167]

The end of the war also brought other, more positive changes for Sada. First, Japan embarked on penicillin production under the guidance of Professor Umezawa Hamao.[168] This miraculous drug freed Sada from the previously inevitable prospect of death and/or insanity resulting from her syphilis. Second, the Japanese Election Law was revised in December 1945, granting women the right to vote in Japan. Women then participated in the April 1946 election, the first general election to be held after the war. Sixty-seven percent of all eligible women voted. Thirty-nine women were elected to the House of Representatives; and for the first time, women comprised 8.4 percent of the lower house of the National Diet of Japan.[169] This signified a changing climate for women in Japan, which made it easier for Japanese society to accept Sada as a victim of male exploitation.[170]

In 1947, what calm and happiness Sada was able to achieve was shattered once again with the release of Kimura Ichiro's book, *Osada iro zange - Abe Sada no kokuhaku* (The Erotic Confessions of Abe Sada). The work became a national bestseller with over 100,000 copies sold. The book was purportedly based on an interview with Sada when in fact it was actually based on the police interrogation records.[171] Yoshii Masako's true identity was revealed and her neighbors in

Saitama pressured her to move away. To make matters worse, her lover was coerced into abandoning her after his friends and family learned the truth.

Sada's notoriety meant that anything bearing her name would become an instant success. Hence, 1947 saw the release of two more publications. In March, Fuyuki Takeshi penned *Aiyoku ni nakinureta onna – Abe Sada no tadotta hansei* (Woman Tearstained in Love – The Life Led by Abe Sada). In August, Funabashi Seiichi published *Abe Sada gyojo-ki* (A Record of Abe Sada's Behavior).[172]

With nowhere else to go, Sada returned to the Inaba household and Masatake once again seized the opportunity to make a profit from her. She joined a theater troupe under the direction of Nagata Mikihiko and portrayed herself in a one-act play called *Showa Ichidai Onna* (A Woman of the Showa Era). Mikihiko was a poet and a playwright who is best known for his 1923 publication, *Daichi wa furu,* a semi-fictional work based on the Great Kanto Earthquake, and for numerous publications dedicated to the Gion district, the most famous geisha district of Kyoto.[173]

The theater troupe toured the country and the advertisements for the play declared that profits from ticket sales would go toward the rehabilitation of female prisoners. In reality, it is not clear how much or whether any of the profits actually went toward that cause. Sada remained with the theater troupe part-time until 1949 while she worked in the *mizu shobai* (water trade).[174] Mizu shobai is a euphemism for the nighttime entertainment business in Japan. It encompasses the hostess or snack bars, bars, and cabarets, and often involves more than serving alcohol to the patrons.

She reverted to using her real name and filed a libel suit against Kimura Ichiro, which was settled out of court. In 1948 she published her own autobiography titled *Abe sada Shouji–ai no hannama* (Memoirs of Abe Sada –half a lifetime spent in love). She attempted to contradict Ichiro's portrayal of her as a sexually depraved individual by emphasizing her love for Kichizo throughout her work. [175]

Also in 1948, a magazine called *Jitsuwa* (True Story) featured previously unpublished photos of the Abe Sada incident with the headline "Ero-guro of the Century! First Public Release. Pictorial of the Abe Sada Incident."[176] *Ero-guro* was short for *Ero guro nansensu*, the name given to the literary and artistic movement that originated in Japan in the 1920s and 1930s. The name is an example of the many *wasei-ego* terms (a combination of English words often abbreviated by the Japanese), which flourished in Japan during the time. This trend of combining and abbreviating English words still continues today in modern-day Japan. *Ero* is an abbreviation of the word erotic and *guro* is an abbreviation of the word grotesque (as in malformed, unnatural, or horrific), while *nansensu* is just the Japanese pronunciation of the word nonsense.

The movement was primarily focused on eroticism, sexual corruption, and decadence and was often characterized as a prewar, bourgeois cultural phenomenon. The Abe Sada incident came to represent and was often associated with that genre for many years to come.[177]

Following the release of her autobiography, Sada was interviewed by a novelist and essayist named Sakaguchi Ango. Ango belonged to a group of young Japanese writers who rose to prominence after World War II with the *Buraiha* (Decadent School). Their work brought to the forefront the aimlessness and the identity crisis that existed in post-World War II Japan.[178]

The interview was published in *Zadan* (Talk) magazine and featured Sada's opinions about female desire, heterosexual love, and the media. He followed up the interview with an essay, in which he called Sada a "tender, warm figure of salvation for future generations."[179] Ango sympathized with her situation and agreed with the logic she had used to kill Kichizo. He also went so far as to say that he had never met a more ordinary woman in his life.[180]

A fellow writer from the *Buraiha*, Oda Sakunosuke, also published two articles about Sada. The first was "Seso" (The State of the Times), published in 1946. The second article was entitled, "Yofu" (The Seductress), and it was published in 1947.

Nagata Mikihiko, the playwright who had previously directed Sada in the one-act stage play, published a serialized novel which ran from September 1950 through August 1951. The publication was called *Jitsuroku: Abe Sada* (True Story: Abe Sada). The title was later changed to *Joen Ichidai Onna* (Impassioned Woman of Love).

Mikihiko's novels were not a re-telling of the Abe Sada incident, but rather a platform through which he attempted to dispel the earlier portrayals of her as a poison woman. The stories unfolded as part of Sada's own narrative and she attempted to normalize sex and the so-called perverse sexual behavior of women. She stated that her behavior was regarded as lascivious only because women were dishonest about their sexual activities. She admonished them for being too restrained in their relationships.[181]

Given the interest that was generated by the Abe Sada incident, it came as no surprise that even Sada's attorney, Takeuchi Kintaro, attempted to profit by publishing his case notes.[182] Sada, on the other hand, was haunted by the stigma of her past and struggled to support herself in a society where economic, social, and cultural barriers relegated her to only certain types of work. Despite it all, she worked hard and at age 54 she received a commendation from the Tokyo Food and Beverage Association recognizing her as an exemplary employee.[183]

Although Sada never pursued fame, she suffered from the disadvantages of her celebrity status following Kichizo's murder. It is safe to assume that she never fully anticipated the economic and psychological impact the incident would have on her life. She was the subject of countless articles, books, and movies, yet she never received royalties from their sales. Also, rather than presenting a true depiction of Abe Sada, these works created a semi-fictionalized persona which mirrored the notions, anxieties, and desires of their creators instead. Sada struggled against this fictitious image, but it was the image which ultimately endured over the years.[184]

After years of living in semi-anonymity and working in bars and restaurants, Sada finally achieved her goal and opened a small restaurant in 1967 called Wakatake. It was an *onigiri* (rice ball) shop located in Taito-ku near the Hibiya Subway line.[185] She continued to live with old friends and acquaintances, and she saved a sizeable sum of money with which she had hoped to open up another business.

However, that dream was shattered when a young man with whom she had a platonic relationship and trusted to become her partner in the new business ran off with her savings. She was forced to close her restaurant in 1970. Once again, she was forced to work as a maid; at a 110-room hotel called Katsuyama. Sada had suffered from rheumatoid arthritis since age sixty, but she continued to work. [186] She worked at Katsuyama for approximately six months and then dropped out of sight completely.[187] When she departed Katsuyama, she left behind a letter. Her letter concluded with the words, "*Watashi wa damena onna* (I am a bad woman.)." She had ended the letters she had written in 1936 prior to her arrest with the same sentence.

There were several rumors which surfaced afterwards stating that she had committed suicide or had entered a convent. None of the rumors were ever confirmed and there is no known record or date of death. Her official family register still indicates that she is alive.[188] Interestingly enough, flowers continued to be left on Ishida Kichizo's grave until 1987.[189]

CHAPTER IX

Legacy

"My greatest regret is that people will misunderstand me and think I'm a lunatic.

With regard to the question of my being a sexual pervert, I think that if you investigate my past you will find a clear answer."

Abe Sada (Interrogation, 1936)[190]

ALTHOUGH ABE SADA was not the only notorious female *satsujin-sha* (murderer) in Japanese history, she did manage to capture the public's attention like no other who came before or after her. She became a popular subject for books, plays, and films in the decades following the incident, and she continues to intrigue and inspire countless others to the present day. In the numerous articles and books written about her, she is often referred to as a *dokufu* (poison-woman).

The term dokufu originated in various dramatic writings during the mid-to-late Tokugawa period and became prevalent during the early Meiji period. It refers to women convicted of vicious crimes and has been used to describe women such as

Takahashi Oden, who was discussed earlier, Yoarashi Okinu, and Hanai Oume.

Yoarashi Okinu, like Sada, was a geisha. She was put to death by beheading in 1872 at Tokyo's *Kozukappara keijo* (Kozukappara execution grounds) after she was charged with poisoning her lover, Kobayashi Kinpei, with arsenic. It was determined that she had killed Kinpei in order to run away with a Kabuki actor named Okada Kikusaburo.

Not much is known about Okinu's earlier life, but what is known is that she was once the mistress of Okubo Tadayori and later abandoned by him. The Okubos were a samurai family who rose to prominence during the Sengoku (Warring States) period through their association with Matsudaira Hirotada, the father of Tokugawa Ieyasu (the founder and first Shogun of the Tokugawa Shogunate). Tadayori was elevated to the rank of *shishaku* (Viscount) sometime during the Meiji period. [191]

On July 7, 1884, the Meiji government adopted the Peerage Act, which was modeled after the British aristocracy. The Act established five titles, and further expanded the hereditary titles of nobility: *koshaku* (公 爵 /Duke), *hoshaku* (侯 爵 /Marquis), *hakushaku* (伯爵/Count), *shishaku* (子爵/Viscount), and *danshaku* (男爵/Baron).[192]

After Tadayori abandoned Okinu, she became the mistress of a man named Kobayashi Kinpei. While she was Kinpei's mistress, she engaged in paid sex with Okada Kikusaburo and in the process she fell in love with him. She became pregnant with Kikusaburo's child, and she and Kikusaburo devised a plan to get Kinpei out of the way.

Following the murder on March 2, 1871, both Okinu and Kikusaburo were arrested. They were both sentenced to death, but because Okinu was pregnant, her execution was delayed until after the birth of her child. Eventually, Kikusaburo's sentence was lessened and he was ordered to serve only three years in prison. Okinu, on the other hand, was beheaded and her head was placed on public display for several days.

Kikusaburo, who had previously been a student of Arashi Rikan III, became a disciple of Ichikawa Danjuro VIII after he finished serving his prison term. He changed his name to Ichikawa Gonjuro and managed to revive his Kabuki career. He remained popular throughout the Meiji period.[193]

Another geisha, Hanai Oume, was arrested and charged with the murder of her male assistant, Minekichi, on June 9, 1887. Like Sada, Oume became a popular subject for the press following her arrest and she went on to publish a book detailing the events leading up to the murder and her time in prison. The book, *Story of Repentance*, propelled Oume to celebrity status.

Oume had been given up for adoption by her biological father when she was eight years old. When she reached the age of fifteen, her adoptive family sold her to an okiya. She eventually became a highly sought-after geisha, and her popularity permitted her to hire a *hakoya* (assistant) to carry her shamisen and various items during working hours. The hakoya was Minekichi.

In 1885, when Oume was twenty-two years old, she went to work in Shinbashi under the alias Hidekichi. She gradually saved enough money, and with the help of a patron she opened an ochaya called Suigetsu on May 14, 1887. However, her patron's insistence on having the ochaya under Oume's biological father's name complicated matters.

Oume's biological father, Sennosuke, who had been absent from his daughter's life after her adoption, now simply wanted to sponge off her success as a geisha and restaurant owner. As he increasingly took over business decisions and treated Oume as a mere employee, she became very resentful. The situation was further exasperated by Minekichi's growing alliance with the overbearing patriarch. Over time, Oume became despondent and attempted to commit suicide by throwing herself into a well. The attempt proved unsuccessful.

Father and daughter continued to argue incessantly about money. Toward the end of May, Sennosuke placed a closed sign on the ochaya's door and locked Oume out of her business. Forced out onto the streets, Oume stayed with acquaintances and strategized about how to get her business back from her father. On June 9, she met with her assistant, Minekichi, and an argument ensued. The situation escalated and Oume, infuriated by Minekichi's boldness, stabbed him in the back with a knife.

She was sentenced to life imprisonment and, like Sada, she was confined to Ichigaya Prison. She was released after the authorities determined that she had been adequately rehabilitated. However, since her lawyers stated during her trial that she suffered from temporary insanity, Oume was haunted in the press for decades by accusations of madness.[194]

Likewise, Sada's trial elevated her to celebrity status, and she inspired countless works to be produced about her. Two of the most notable films about Sada's life were released in the mid-1970s following her disappearance from the public eye.

The first was a Nikkatsu Roman Porno film called *Jitsuroku Abe Sada* (*Recorded Actual Facts Abe Sada*) with the English title *A Woman Called Abe Sada*). Directed by Tanaka Noboru, it was released on February 8, 1975.

Noboru was born in the village of Hakuba in Nagano prefecture on August 15, 1937. During the time of his birth the Second Sino-Japanese War in China was already underway, and Abe Sada was serving the first year of her six year sentence in Tochigi. Noboru graduated from Meiji University with a major in French Literature and had aspirations of becoming a novelist. However, his interests later turned to poetry and he became interested in films as a means for expressing his poetic thoughts.[195]

Jitsuroku Abe Sada starred the then twenty-six-year-old Miyashita Junko as Sada and a forty-year-old actor named Esumi Hideaki as Kichizo.[196] Junko was a former waitress who was recruited to work in *Pinku eiga* (Pink films—Japanese films with sexual content or nudity). After making her debut in 1971, she enjoyed a career that spanned four decades and included over 160 films.[197]

Nikkatsu Roman Porno was an old, obscene genre of filmmaking that was introduced by the Nikkatsu Studio when it was facing bankruptcy in the 1970s due to the influx of Western films and the emergence of television. This explicit genre of film was created to generate box office profits during a time when the only other income generating Japanese films were produced for children. The Roman Porno films were often low-budget, softcore flicks shot during a span of one week, and featured nudity or sex scenes every 10 to 15 minutes.[198]

Jitsuroku Abe Sada tells a highly fictionalized story of Abe Sada's life through a series of flashbacks. Although Tanaka Noboru's movie was erotic, it did not cross the line into pornography and was spared by Japanese censorship. While Article 21 of the Japanese Constitution guarantees freedom of expression and prohibits formal censorship, Article 175 of Japan's Criminal Code mandates censorship of all work that is deemed to be pornographic in nature.[199]

The second, and probably the most well-known film about Abe Sada, was directed by the famed Japanese film director and screenwriter, Oshima Nagisa. *Ai no Korida* (English title: *In the Realm of the Senses*, French title: *L'Empire des sens*) was released in 1976 and is often the movie that most people refer to and base their knowledge on when discussing the subject of Abe Sada.

Ai no Korida featured a twenty-four-year-old actress named Matsuda Eiko as Sada and a thirty-five-year-old actor named Fuji Tatsuya as Kichizo. Unlike the Tanaka film, this dramatized story of the Abe Sada incident pushed the boundaries between art and pornography by utilizing scenes with actual sexual activity between the actors, thus embroiling the director in deep controversy.

But controversy was nothing new to Nagisa. After majoring in political history at Kyoto University, he worked for the Shochiku Limited film production company. His cinematic career developed quickly, and in 1960 he directed the controversial film, *Nihon no Yoru to Kiri* (*Night and Fog in Japan*). The film expressed the director's disillusionment with traditional politics in Japan and consequently was pulled from circulation after just one week. The production company believed that the film would create unrest in light of Yamaguchi Otoya's recent assassination of Asanuma Inejiro.

Inejiro was the leader of the Japanese Socialist Party and was known for his forceful advocacy of socialism in post-war Japan and his open criticism of U.S.–Japanese relations. He was slain with a *yoroi-doshi* (a traditional Japanese sword that was worn by the samurai class) by Otoya while he was speaking at a nationally televised political debate in Tokyo. His violent death was broadcast in graphic detail and caused widespread shock and outrage.[200]

Having his film pulled from circulation enraged Nagisa, and he left the studio and started his own independent production company. Ironically, *Nihon no Yoru to Kiri* placed tenth in that year's *Kinema Junpo's* Best Films poll. Kinema Junpo is Japan's oldest and premiere cinema magazine. Once every ten years, it polls Japanese critics to name the best Japanese films of all time.[201]

The sexually explicit scenes in *Ai no Korida* meant that the film could not be produced as a Japanese movie; therefore, it was officially designated as a joint Japanese and French production. The scenes were shot in Japan and the film was shipped to France for developing and editing. Still, *Ai no Korida* was banned in many countries and Nagisa faced an obscenity trial in Japan once the script and movie stills were published. He was acquitted after the jury was reportedly left speechless when Nagisa challenged them to describe what they found to be obscene in the film. The movie was screened in Japan only after it had undergone strict editing.

Whether it was a publicity stunt or not, Nagisa allegedly tracked Sada down while he was preparing to shoot *Ai no Korida*. She was purported to have been in her late sixties at the time and was living in a nunnery located in a rural part of Kansai.[202]

In 1969, Sada herself appeared in a film called *Meiji, Taisho Showa: Ryoki onna hanzai-shi (English title: Love and Crime)* directed by Ishii Teruo.[203]

Teruo was born in Sada's beloved Asakusa neighborhood on January 1, 1924. As a young boy, his parents took him to see all of the foreign films that were popular in Japan at the time. This experience contributed to his great love of cinema later in life. Teruo entered the movie business in 1942 as an assistant director for Toho Studios, but his career was interrupted when he was sent to Manchuria during World War II to take aerial photographs for bombing raids. After the war, Teruo returned to filmmaking and became known for his many films in the Ero-guro genre.[204]

Meiji, Taisho Showa: Ryoki onna hanzai-shi featured a series of short stories about bizarre crimes committed by women during the Meiji (1868 – 1912), Taisho (1912 – 1926), and Showa (1926–1989) eras. Sada portrayed herself in the 1969 segment of "Abe Sada jiken" ("Abe Sada Incident"). The younger, 1936 version of Sada was portrayed by a twenty-one-year-old actress named Kagawa Yukie.[205]

In 1983, Sada's name was used in yet another Roman Porno film directed by Sugano Takashi called *Sexy Doll: Abe Sada Sansei*. The movie capitalized on Sada's name although the story had nothing to do with her.

In 1994, Japanese musician Akita Masami, the founder of Merzbow, released an EP (extended play) album under the alias Abe Sada. The two-track album entitled *Original Body Kingdom/Gala Abe Sada 1936* was his only release under the alias.[206]

In 1997, Japanese author Watanabe Junichi penned a novel called *Shitsurakuen* (*A Lost Paradise*). *Shitsurakuen* told the story of a 54-year-old married former magazine editor named Kuki and his affair with a 37-year-old married typesetter named Rinko. The couple were modeled after Sada and Kichizo, and similarly their burning passion eventually destroyed them. The book sold three million copies in Japan and became a national bestseller.

The novel inspired a film by the same name, which was released in May of 1997. The film was directed by Morita Yoshimitsu and starred the then 41-year-old Yakusho Koji as

Kuki and 37-year-old Kuroki Hitomi as Rinko. The film earned Koji the Japan Academy Prize for Outstanding Performance by an Actor in a Leading Role in 1998.

In 1998, Horinouchi Masakazu published a 438-page biography of Abe Sada entitled *Abe Sada seiden*. The author is known for his biographical work, including the 2003 publication *Sogen no hito: Misora Hibari kara no tegami* (*Letters from Misora Hibari*). Misora Hibari was a Japanese singer, actress, and cultural icon born in Yokohama in 1937. She was awarded the Japanese Medal of Honor for her contributions to music and for giving the public hope and encouragement after World War II.

This was the same year during which Obayashi Nobuhiko's film *Sada: Gesaku: Abe Sada no shogai* was released. Kuroki Hitomi, the actress who portrayed Rinko in the film version of *A Lost Paradise*, depicted Sada, and Kataoka Tsurutaro played the part of her ill-fated lover, Kikumoto Tatsuzo. Despite the fact that Kichizo's name and certain key factors in the story were altered, the film was the first to take a less explicit approach in recounting the events leading up to the infamous incident. Rather than focusing on the sexually explicit nature of the topic, as others before him had done, the director attempted to uncover Sada's true motives.

In March 2007, Sada's name was used by an Australian sound artist and composer, Cat Hope, to found a bass orchestra project. Their debut album *Subzilla* was followed by two other releases in 2009 and 2010. In 2016, three musicians from Ohio formed a rock/metal/alternative metal band called Sada Abe.[207]

Most recently, Yokosuka-born manga artist, Kamimura Kazuo, along with Okazaki Hideo and Togawa Masako, produced a two-volume manga called *Sada Abe*, which was released strictly for the German market in 2018.

Even though it has been well over eighty years since the Abe Sada incident first captured the attention and the imagination of the public, it still continues to fascinate and provoke scandal-hungry audiences all over the world. The stories may deviate somewhat from the actual facts pertaining to Sada's life and her crime, but the intrigue created by the incident all those years ago still feeds the creative minds of those who endeavor to convey her story. Sada may have faded from the public eye in the 1970s, but the public's interest in her most certainly has not.

Postscript

REGARDLESS OF HOW often Sada's story is retold, one thing remains constant, and that is the steady focus on her sexuality. Starting with the newspaper articles, which sensationalized the trial in the 1930s, the numerous works which emerged following the murder focused more on Sada and Kichizo's sexual relationship than the circumstances of Sada's life which led to the tragic end of her lover. Oftentimes, these works conveyed in great detail Sada's lovemaking with Kichizo, and devoted very little effort to actually describing and analyzing the circumstances under which she was raised, lived, and survived.

One possible reason for this may be that the majority of these works were produced by men and they reflected the predominant male perspective in Japan's patriarchal society. Or, it could simply be a result of the old adage that sex sells— and we know that anything to which Sada's name was attached sold successfully.

If we focus on the impact of the fundamental views of its patriarchal society, we can agree that despite the various women's liberation movements that have surfaced over the years, attitudes toward women and their roles in society have changed very little in Japan. Furthermore, given Japan's neophobic nature and adherence to traditionalism, the prevailing attitudes toward women will more than likely remain unchanged in the years to come.

The Meiji Restoration in 1868 gave rise to a series of events that could have served as catalysts for altering social views toward women, had it not been for the government's widespread efforts to preserve patriarchal hegemony. The first such event involved the Meiji government's move toward cultivating Japanese girls in Western ways, grooming them to become models of ideal womanhood to help usher in a new and modernized Japanese nation. The second was the freedom granted to average citizens to voice their opinions in public for the first time, which engendered the first People's Rights Movement. Among the movement's advocates were a small group of women who called for *danjo doken* (male–female equal rights) and *joken* (women's rights). Fearful of the consequences of permitting such a movement to gain a foothold, the government quickly imposed press censorship laws and restricted verbal expression during the early decades of the Meiji period. This enabled the government to clamp down on the leading feminists of the time.[208]

One such person was an orator named Kishida Toshiko. Previously the lady-in-waiting to Empress Haruko, she left her job to tour the nation, delivering lectures to predominantly female audiences. She used her lectures to criticize the marriage system in which women had no right to divorce, the concubine system in which men could have multiple wives, and the lack of educational opportunities for girls. She attacked the traditional Confucian values in which women were under the control of their fathers, husbands, or sons throughout their lives.[209]

These traditional Confucian values were still upheld during the end of the Taisho era (1912- 1926), when a girl like Sada could be sold into the sex industry by her father without discourse. Furthermore, it was mandated that a male representative intervene on a woman's behalf when it came to finding a job, whether the job happened to be within the sex industry, the factories, or the restaurants. Women simply were not given the right to act on their own and in their own self-interest.

In 1883, after delivering a speech entitled "Daughters in Boxes," Toshiko was arrested and fined. The boxes in Toshiko's speech represented the emotional and physical limitations placed on young girls by their families. One box represented the girls who were confined to their rooms and not allowed to have any contact with the outside world. Another box represented the girls who were expected to be obedient to their parents despite never having received any love or affection from them. The last box represented educating and empowering women through knowledge, and this was the box Toshiko valued the most.

She proclaimed that in a civilized culture, women were regarded as equals in both society and within the family. She further went on to say that if Japan were to attain gender equality it would most definitely elevate the nation's status in the international arena. Naturally, the Meiji reformers, despite all of their efforts to change Japanese society for the better, were not ready for someone, particularly a woman, to challenge the cultural norms of Japanese society. In response, they passed the Peace Preservation Law in 1887, which prohibited women from publicly engaging in political activity. Consequently, Toshiko was forced to abandon her public speaking engagements, but she continued to inspire other feminists through her articles published in *Jogaku Zasshi*. *Jogaku Zasshi*, a magazine which was first published in 1885, played a leading role in helping to create the model of the modern Japanese women.[210]

One of Toshiko's notable disciples was Fukuda Hideko. Once regarded as someone who was resistant to conforming to "proper" feminine behavior, she went on to establish a private all-girls school. Sadly, the school was shut down by the government in 1884 due to concerns over the growing number of women who exhibited political ambitions. Although the Meiji government had promoted girls' education, the curricula they supported did not emphasize the development of women's intelligence and personality, but rather trained women to be obedient to their husbands and raise children. The shutting down of her school did not stop Hideko, however, and she became the founding editor of the feminist newspaper *Seikai Fujin* (*Women of the World*) in 1907.[211]

Other feminists followed and struggled for decades to improve conditions through their activism in transnational organizations. For instance, the Japanese branch of the International Woman's Christian Temperance Union worked tirelessly to end international sex trafficking, licensed prostitution, and marital inequality, but women's legal status remained significantly inferior to men's through the pre–World War II era.

Following the end of World War II, a new Constitution was adopted granting equal rights to all citizens. The a new Civil Code followed that eradicated most of the patriarchal provisions of the 1898 civil code, and a Labor Standards Law came into existence which proscribed equal pay for equal work. Nevertheless, Japanese women continued to face discrimination through the legal system, in the workplace, and at home.[212]

Japan has indisputably been a patriarchy both historically and culturally, leaving few viable options for women not only to survive, but to succeed and to thrive. Unfortunately, the problems of misogyny are spread deep and wide throughout Japanese culture and society, where a woman is punished merely for being a woman.

There is an old Japanese saying, *Suezen kuwanu wa otoko no haji* (It is a man's dishonor not to partake in what is offered to him on a platter). In other words, it is disgraceful for a man to refuse a woman who offers herself to him. Suezen basically means a meal set before a person. Consequently, adultery and infidelity have always been time-honored Japanese traditions—for the nation's men.

There has been and continues to be a wide array of options for Japanese men who want to have an affair or a sexual experience outside of marriage and with no strings attached. As a result, the sex industry has always thrived in Japan, even after the passage of the Prostitution Prevention Law in 1956. As a matter of fact, the male-centered sex industry currently accounts for two percent of Japan's gross domestic product.[213] In examining Sada's situation, we can see that the majority of the men with whom she had affairs were married. Furthermore, it is safe to assume that a large percentage of her clients were also married when she worked as a geisha and a prostitute.

This is not to say that Japanese wives do not have affairs, as was the case with Kichizo's own wife; she ran off with her lover, leaving behind her husband and children for a year. It is just that the wives typically tend to be more discreet. For example, a 2008 poll conducted by The Ministry of Health, Labor and Welfare disclosed that among married men between the ages of 16 and 49, twenty percent admitted to have had an extramarital affair compared to eleven percent of the women in the same category.[214] Adultery and the success of the sex industry in Japan are further aided by the fact that women are often forced to give up working and a considerable portion of their independence to stay at home and raise a family. Dependent on their husbands for their economic survival, the women often turn a blind eye to their husbands' infidelity. This old, chauvinistic belief that a woman's place is in the home is still prevalent today, although Japan is recognized as one of the most advanced, affluent, and democratic countries in the world. Women continue to be repressed, kept on the margins of society, business, and politics while society clings to centuries-old traditions.

A recent example of Japanese society's reluctance to abandon old, outdated customs which discriminate against women came to light through a series of events which unfolded on April 4, 2018. On this day, the 66-year-old Maizuru Mayor, Tatami Ryozo, suddenly collapsed while delivering a speech during a sumo exhibition in Kyoto. Several men rushed to the *dohyo* (ring) to aid him, but it was clear that they were at a loss over what to do. Immediately afterwards, a female nurse came up from the audience and started administering cardiopulmonary resuscitation to the mayor. Her actions and the actions of several other women who joined her in the ring to assist the stricken mayor sparked a national debate on the controversial traditions of the sumo world.

During the time when the women were aiding the mayor, a sumo official repeatedly ordered them to leave the ring. His actions were in adherence to the centuries-old sumo tradition banning women from entering the sacred ring. The ban is based on Shinto and Buddhist beliefs that consider women to be impure because of menstrual blood. The situation generated condemnation from the foreign media who saw it as a sign of women's relatively low social status in male-dominated Japan.[215]

In August of 2018, Tokyo Medical University officials admitted that the test scores of qualified female prospective students were deliberately altered to limit their acceptance in favor of admitting less qualified male students. In addition, according to findings released by lawyers involved in the investigation, Tokyo Medical University manipulated entrance exam results starting in 2006, and possibly even earlier.

Japanese society's expectation is that women will quit work once they are married or become pregnant, and that excuse has conveniently been used to justify keeping them out of career-track positions and relegating them to menial, low level jobs with little or no chance of promotion.

In May of 2019, Emperor Akihito abdicated, allowing his son Naruhito to ascend the throne. During the ascension ceremony, which dates back thousands of years, the new Empress Masako, Naruhito's wife of 26 years, was not allowed to attend.

The rules of protocol which pertain to Japan's monarchy were enacted during the Meiji era. They specify that women in the royal family are not permitted to be in the room when the new emperor receives the sacred regalia signifying his rightful succession. These same rules also prohibit women from reigning and stipulate that women born into the royal family must officially leave it once they marry.

Although, for the first time in history, Katayama Satsuki, a female member of Prime Minister Abe Shinzo's cabinet was allowed to witness the ceremony, conservatives continued to underscore the importance of tradition to justify keeping women from participating in sacred ceremonies and out of the line of succession. In an interview given to *The New York Times*, Professor Yagi Hidetsugu from the Reitaku University in Kashiwa stated, "If a female or the child of a female royal succeeds to the throne, it would be a major change. The imperial family would lose its legitimacy." Conversely, the associate professor of cultural and historical studies at Otemae University in Nishinomiya, Tanaka Kathryn, stated "This is not about 'tradition,' but rather reflects specific political and patriarchal world views."[216]

Japan continues to be out of step with regard to gender equality through its objectification of women. This is clearly evidenced in sociologist Karen Shire's research, which focuses on the hiring practices of Japanese companies. Her research demonstrates that hiring managers often focus on a potential female employee's grooming and temperament in direct contrast to the managers' focus on the decision-making and analytical styles of potential male candidates.[217]

It is clear that the male dominated, misogynistic society that existed during Abe Sada's time is still alive and well in modern Japan, and it will probably continue to exist in the decades to come.

This was the society which labeled Abe Sada as a sexually immoral individual and blamed her almost entirely for the direction that her life had taken. Few people, if any, dared to question the society that pushed a woman to make the choices that Abe Sada had made in her life.

Author William Johnston called attention to this fact when he wrote, "Abe claimed that she had committed murder in order to establish the same right over a man that men had over women, and thus emphasized the gender-based disempowerment of women in contemporary Japanese society."[218]

While society as a whole was reluctant to acknowledge its responsibility for creating the circumstances which caused women like Sada to be pushed to the corner, the nation's past and present fascination with the Abe Sada incident is quite telling. Why did so many young women fanatically follow her trial? Also, why has Sada's story so often been romanticized?

One possible answer could be that Sada and her actions represent the repressed emotions of countless Japanese women who have found themselves hindered and exploited. In a society where the law does little to protect women against exploitation and where there is significant cultural pressure to accept and bear hardship, many young women who felt vulnerable might have perceived Sada and her actions as empowering. Their support of her, both as a victim and an aggressor, may be viewed as a silent protest against a society that has treated them unfairly.

Time and time again, both through her detailed testimony and her memoirs, Sada emphasized that she had killed Kichizo out of love. She loved him so obsessively that she wanted nothing more than to dominate him and make him exclusively hers.

In contrast, similar crimes committed by women before and after the Abe Sada incident were all seemingly motivated by hatred. Takahashi Oden allegedly poisoned her husband and ruthlessly slit her lover's throat, leaving him to die in his own pool of blood. Yoarashi Okinu poisoned her lover so that she could run away with the actor she had fallen in love with. Hanai Oume killed a man for supporting her overbearing parent. These were all women who in some way were exploited by men.

In recent times, in another high-profile case that captivated the media, Kakehi Chisako (dubbed the Black Widow by the Japanese media) claimed that she wanted to kill her husband out of deep hatred.

Kakehi Chisako was born Yamamoto Chisako on November 28, 1946, to a middle-class family in Kitakyushu City, Fukuoka prefecture. She reportedly was a good student and had ambitions to attend university, but her traditionalist father, who deemed it improper for a girl to pursue higher education, did not allow her to do so.

Acquiescing to her father's wishes, Chisako worked as a bank teller from 1965 until 1969, when she married her first husband. He was a successful entrepreneur who ran a fabric-printing company, with whom she had two children. In 1994, at the age of fifty-four, he suddenly suffered a heart attack and was rushed to the hospital. He died on the very night he was to be discharged.

Just one year after her first husband's death, Chisako married a man who managed a wholesale pharmaceutical firm. In 2006, when he was sixty-nine years old, he suffered a stroke and passed away.

In 2007, Chisako became engaged to a man in his seventies named Suehiro Toshiaki. He was a former prefectural official from Kobe. Shortly after their engagement, Toshiaki collapsed in the middle of a busy street near the JR Motomachi Station in Kobe. He remained on life support until June 2009, when he seemingly passed away from cancer.[219]

In February 2008, Chisako married her third husband, 75-year-old Yamamoto Toshiaki. He successfully managed an agricultural cooperative. Just three months after their marriage, Toshiaki passed away from a heart attack.

In September 2011, Chisako became engaged again, this time to 71-year-old Honda Masanori. Six months later, Masanori passed away while he was riding his motorcycle. The cause of death was attributed to cardiac arrhythmia.

It wasn't long before Chisako became involved with a 75-year-old retired architect named Hioki Minoru. Following dinner on September 20, 2013, Minoru collapsed and died. At the time, the cause of death was believed to have been lung cancer.[220]

Just weeks later, Chisako married her fourth husband, 75-year-old Kakehi Isao. He was found dead in his home in Muko City, Kyoto on December 28, 2013. Chisako was arrested in November, 2014, after an autopsy conducted on Isao revealed traces of cyanide poisoning. At the time of her arrest, she had been seeing two other men, who were warned by police to end their relationships with her.

Chisako met her various partners through matchmaking agencies. As a matter of fact, she was a member of at least ten different matchmaking agencies in various prefectures. Her requirements for a prospective spouse were very clear; he must be elderly, childless, a homeowner, and (ideally) wealthy. All in all, Chisako had been romantically linked to between seven and fourteen men. She managed to convince all of them to make her the sole beneficiary of their assets. In doing so, she amassed the equivalent of at least $8.8 million in insurance and inheritance payouts, which she squandered away on failed investments.

Following her arrest, the police became suspicious of the earlier deaths, but those suspicions were impossible to prove since the bodies had been cremated. They were, however, able to obtain a sample of Suehiro Toshiaki's blood from the hospital where he had passed away. As they had suspected, the sample contained traces of cyanide.[221]

Chisako's high-profile trial lasted 135 days, and it was determined that she had killed her partners with health cocktails that had been laced with cyanide, a chemical she was familiar with from her first husband's fabric-printing business. She initially pleaded not guilty, but later confessed on the witness stand that she "had no intention of hiding the guilt" and "wanted to kill out of deep hatred."[222] She also stated that she had killed her fourth husband, Isao, because he was discriminating against her by financially supporting another woman while they were married. The other woman was someone Isao had previously dated.

Two days after her confession, Chisako retracted her statement and claimed to not remember having said it. Ultimately, she was charged with three counts of murder and one count of attempted murder and sentenced to death by hanging. During her sentencing hearing she told the judges, "Even if I were executed tomorrow, I would die smiling."[223]

With very little information available about her early life, it is difficult to determine whether Chisako's misandry stemmed from any hatred she may have harbored toward her controlling father, who denied her the opportunity to pursue higher education, or whether it was due to any other acts of repression or exploitation she may have experienced at the hands of the men with whom she worked with at the bank. What is known is that she showed no remorse for her actions.

Although Sada's crime was premeditated and just as heinous as the others, her case was rather unique in that it was not motivated by hatred, financial gain, or the desire to end her relationship with Kichizo. Perhaps this is the singular reason why her story has so often been romanticized and retold in various formats.

Sada's story, in some ways, represents the attempt of a repressed woman to assert herself in a society that continually subjected her to the will and the whim of the men who surrounded her. Her desire to control someone seemingly arose from having been objectified and controlled all of her life. That control was not just limited to the men in her life: her father, the man who raped her, and the countless men who profited off of her. Sada was also used and controlled by her mother, who wanted to live her life through her youngest daughter. Rather than producing a hateful, misandristic individual, these experiences left Sada with a strong need to be loved and genuinely cared for.

Unfortunately, this unfulfilled need left her vulnerable to exploitation. Time and time again, her trust was betrayed and her sense of self-worth was stripped away, layer by layer. As a result, she developed an obsessive devotion to those who showed her kindness and treated her well, namely Omiya Goro and Ishida Kichizo.

Despite his sexual involvement with Sada, Goro was perhaps the only man in her life who did not merely want to take advantage of her sexually and/or financially. During their various meetings, he showed concern for her health and well-being, and demonstrated a genuine interest in her future. He assisted her financially and was fully prepared to help her leave the sex industry and establish herself as a legitimate business owner. In a sense, the older Goro was the ideal father figure that Sada so desperately wanted and needed. It is not surprising that she hesitated to end her relationship with him after she became romantically involved with Kichizo. Goro did not satisfy her sexually, but he did fulfill her need to have someone reliable to turn to in times of need. The only thing that Sada could offer him in return was her body. On the face of it, the only way she knew how to interact with men was through sex.

Kichizo, on the other hand, was able to satisfy Sada sexually. And even more importantly, he put her needs ahead of his own when they were together. For Sada, after having slept with countless men for money, the idea of a man making her feel important was new and exhilarating.

While Kasahara Kinnosuke described her as a slut and a whore, Kichizo did things to make her happy. Her encounters with him were perhaps the only time in her life when she came close to knowing what love truly felt like—and she grew obsessively jealous.

This made her become irrational and have obsessive thoughts about Kichizo's possible sexual unfaithfulness, either with his wife or with other women. Having been abandoned numerous times in her life, Sada's anxiety was deeply instilled in her. As a consequence, she feared losing Kichizo and/or being abandoned by him.

According to an article published by the IPITIA (the Institut Psicològic Internacional), Sada's behavior can be classified as a textbook case of obsessive jealousy. The IPITIA states that obsessive jealousy can often manifest in individuals who have been exposed to rigid and controlling education, as well as traumatic experiences. Other important factors attributable to the condition are a very rigid upbringing, as well as a lack of affection and positive reinforcement. The IPITIA adds that oftentimes the parents of the individual who exhibits obsessive jealousy tend to be misogynistic. In this type of family, the father role is often absent and compensated for by an excessively controlling mother. The mother is frequently in a depressive and/or anxious state and demonstrates a strong dependency and emotional attachment to her children. This typically causes the children to develop an extreme need for attention.[224]

Individuals who exhibit obsessive jealousy live with a constant sense of emptiness, which leads them to a process of over adaptation. By definition, over adaptation is a passive behavior in which the person complies with what he or she believes are the wishes of others, without checking and without reference to his or her own wishes.[225]

Over adaptation tends to cause dependency because it makes the over adapter feel good. The relationship ends up being the central part of the over adapter's life and their main source of happiness and fulfillment. It is also common for the person who suffers from obsessive jealousy to have a strong temperament and a strong sex drive.[226]

In light of all of these factors, it is both unfair and irresponsible to merely focus on Sada as a sex industry worker who committed a heinous crime and disregard the circumstances that drove her to the point of murder. In a society where women are seldom given a voice, her actions come across as a powerful commentary against repression and exploitation.

Sadly, it may not be possible to view the story of Abe Sada without prejudice until society evolves beyond treating women as second-class citizens and embraces and values the potential and contributions of women at home, at work, and socially. This can only be achieved if gender equality is championed by both men and women.

Notes

[1] **Narayan, S.** "Women in Meiji Japan: Exploring the Underclass of Japanese Industrialization." Inquiries Journal/Student Pulse. http://www.inquiriesjournal.com/articles/1369/women-in-Meiji-japan-exploring-the-underclass-of-Japanese-industrialization.

[2] **Sanderson, Beck.** *Ethics of Civilization (Volume 21) East Asia 1800-1949.* "Japan's Modernization 1800-1894." World Peace Communications, 2007. http://www.san.beck.org/21-7-JapanModernization1800-94.html.

[3] **Narayan,** "Women in Meiji Japan."

[4] **Robins-Mowry, Dorothy.** *The Hidden Sun: Women of Modern Japan.* Westview Press, 1983. Page 36.

[5] **Narayan.** "Women in Meiji Japan."

[6] **Hoffman, Michael.** "The rarely, if ever, told story of Japanese sold as slaves by Portuguese traders." *The Japan Times.* May 26, 2013.

[7] ***Monumenta Nipponica: Studies on Japanese Culture, Past and Present***, Volume 59, Issues 3-4. Jochi Daigaku (Sophia University), 2004. Page 463.

[8] **Weiner, Michael,** ed. *Race, Ethnicity and Migration in Modern Japan: Imagined and imaginary minorities.* Taylor & Francis, 2004. Page 408.

[9] ***Monumenta Nipponica.***

[10] **Moran, J. F.** *The Japanese and the Jesuits: Alessandro Valignano in Sixteenth Century Japan,* 1st Edition. "The Japanese Jesuits." Routledge, 1993. Pages 384-386.

[11] **Dias, Maria Suzette Fernandes.** *Legacies of slavery: comparative perspectives.* Cambridge Scholars Publishing, 2007. Page 238.

[12] **Narayan.** "Women in Meiji Japan."

[13] **Ibid.**

[14] **Ibid.**

[15] **Ibid.**

[16] **"Infanticide in Japan: Sign of the Times?"** *The New York Times.* December 8, 1973.

[17] **Norgren, Tiana.** *Abortion before Birth Control: The Politics of Reproduction in Postwar Japan.* Princeton University Press, 2001. Pages 22-23.

[18] **Prostitute Emancipation Act.** Samurai-Archives, 2014, wiki.samurai-archives.com/index.php?title=Prostitute_Emancipation_Act.

[19] **Narayan.** "Women in Meiji Japan."

[20] Anderson, Patricia. "Roles of Samurai Women: Social Norms and Inner Conflicts During Japan's Tokugawa Period, 1603-1868." New Views on Gender, Volume 15 (February, 2015). Pages 30-37.

[21] **Narayan.** "Women in Meiji Japan."

[22] Ibid.

[23] **Stephenson, Andrea Lind.** *Culture of Desire: The History and Development of Sexual Services in Japan* (thesis). Skemman, 7 May 2018. Skemman.is/handle/1946/30004. Page 9.

[24] Ibid.

[25] **Johnston, William.** *Geisha, Harlot, Strangler, Star: A Woman, Sex, and Morality in Modern Japan.* Columbia University Press, 2005. Page 168.

[26] "Perry Expedition." Wikipedia. https://en.wikipedia.org/wiki/Perry_Expedition.

[27] **前坂 俊之 (Abe Sada)** 阿部定手記—愛の半生 (*Abe sada shuki – ai no hansei (Memoirs of Sada Abe)*). Chuokoron-sha, Inc., 1948. Page 33.

[28] **Kapur, Roshni.** "Welcome to the Family: Adult Adoptions in Corporate Japan." Rappler, 2016. www.rappler.com/world/regions/asia-pacific/119305-japan-adult-male-adoption.

[29] **Ravina, Mark.** *The Last Samurai: The Life and Battles of Saigo Takamori.* John Wiley & Sons, 2011. Page 157.

[30] **Ishimaru, Yasko.** "Omiai". John Hopkins University. faculty.tru.ca/jhu/Omiai.pdf. September 2003.

[31] **Johnston, William.** *Geisha, Harlot, Strangler, Star.* Page 21.

[32] **前坂 俊之.** (Abe Sada). Page 32.

[33] **Kosumikku Intanashonaru.** *Abe Sada: Jiken chosho zenbun": Inochi kezuru seiai no onna* (Japanese Edition). [Police Investigation Report- Full Text]. January 1, 1997. Page 13.

[34] **Johnston, William.** *Geisha, Harlot, Strangler, Star.* Page 168.

[35] "Kanda, Tokyo." Wikipedia, https://en.wikipedia.org/wiki/Kanda,_Tokyo.

[36] "Yamanote and Shitamachi." Wikipedia. https://en.wikipedia.org/wiki/Yamanote_and_Shitamachi.

[37] "Taikomochi-the Male Geisha." h2g2 The Hitchhiker's Guide to the Galaxy: Earth Edition (June 23, 2014). h2g2.com/edited_entry/A87805623.

[38] Ibid.

[39] Ibid.

[40] Ibid.

[41] Ibid.

[42] **前坂 俊之 (Abe Sada).** Pages 13-14.

[43] Ibid. Pages 15-16.

[44] **Johnston, William.** *Geisha, Harlot, Strangler, Star.* Page 165.

[45] **前坂 俊之 (Abe Sada).** Pages 16-17.

[46] **Johnston, William.** *Geisha, Harlot, Strangler, Star.* Page 46.

[47] **Yamamoto, Mari** and **Jake Adelstein**. "Does Japan Ever Convict Men for Rape?" The Daily Beast, The Daily Beast Company, 11 May 2017. www.thedailybeast.com/does-japan-ever-convict-men-for-rape.

[48] **Johnston, William**. *Geisha, Harlot, Strangler, Star*. Page 26.

[49] **前坂 俊之** (Abe Sada). Page 16.

[50] **Johnston, William**. *Geisha, Harlot, Strangler, Star*. Page 172.

[51] "Asakusa: The Heart of Old Tokyo." JAPANISTRY, 6 Aug. 2018. www.japanistry.com/asakusa//.

[52] "Denkikan." Wikipedia, www.en.m.wikipedia.org/wiki/Denkikan.

[53] **前坂 俊之** (Abe Sada). Page 17.

[54] **Horinouchi, Masakazu**. 阿部定正伝 (*Abe Sada seiden*). 東京: 情報センター出版局, 1998. Page 18.

[55] *The Culture of Japan as Seen Through Its Leisure*, Linhard, Sepp and Fruhstuck, Sabine (eds.). State University of New York Press, 1998. Page 281.

[56] **前坂 俊之** (Abe Sada). Page 20.

[57] **Johnston, William**. *Geisha, Harlot, Strangler, Star*. Page 54-61.

[58] **前坂 俊之** (Abe Sada). Page 21.

[59] "Tokyo-Yokohama earthquake of 1923." Encyclopaedia Britannica, https://www.britannica.com/event/Tokyo-Yokohama-earthquake-of-1923.

[60] **前坂 俊之** (Abe Sada). Page 22.

[61] **Johnston, William**. *Geisha, Harlot, Strangler, Star*. Page 63-66.

[62] **Horinouchi, Masakazu**. 阿部定正伝 (*Abe Sada seiden*). Pages 334-338.

[63] **Johnston, William**. *Geisha, Harlot, Strangler, Star*. Page 63-66.

[64] **Tull, Matthew, and Steven Gans**. "Symptoms of PTSD After a Rape." Verywell Mind. www.verywellmind.com/symptoms-of-ptsd-after-a-rape-2797203.

[65] **Cichocki, Mark, and Susan Olender**. "Get Familiar with the Symptoms of Syphilis." Verywell Health, Verywellhealth. www.verywellhealth.com/syphilis-signs-and-symptoms-49530.

[66] **Johnston, William**. *Geisha, Harlot, Strangler, Star*. Page 173.

[67] **前坂 俊之** (Abe Sada). Page 23.

[68] **Johnston, Eric**. "Love Town Where Time Stands Still." *The Japan Times*, 2001. www.japantimes.co.jp/community/2001/07/08/general/love-town-where-time-stands-still/#.XFN3tM2IY2w.

[69] "Tobita Shinchi." Wikipedia. https://en.wikipedia.org/wiki/Tobita_Shinchi.

[70] **Johnston, William**. *Geisha, Harlot, Strangler, Star*. Page 68.

[71] "Arsphenamine." Wikipedia.
https://en.wikipedia.org/wiki/Arsphenamine.

[72] **Boskey, Elizabeth,** and **Susan Olender.** "Is It Possible to Get the Same STD Twice?" Verywell Health, Verywellhealth. www.verywellhealth.com/can-i-get-the-same-std-a-second-time-3133003.

[73] **前坂 俊之** (Abe Sada). Page 27.

[74] **Johnston, William.** *Geisha, Harlot, Strangler, Star.* Page 181-182.

[75] **前坂 俊之** (Abe Sada). Page 29.

[76] **Ibid.** Page 30.

[77] **Johnston, William.** *Geisha, Harlot, Strangler, Star.* Page 207.

[78] **前坂 俊之** (Abe Sada). Page 29.

[79] "What Is Dotonbori?" The Official Web Site [of] The Shopping District of Dotonbori. www.dotonbori.or.jp/en/about/index.html.

[80] "The Takarazuka Revue's Allure." TAKARAZUKA REVUE Official Website. kageki.hankyu.co.jp/English/about/index.html.

[81] **Johnston, William.** *Geisha, Harlot, Strangler, Star.* Page 208.

[82] Ibid. Page 75.

[83] Ibid. Page 76.

[84] **前坂 俊之** (Abe Sada). Page 31.

[85] "Rikken Seiyūkai." Wikipedia.
https://en.wikipedia.org/wiki/Rikken_Seiy%C5%ABkai.

[86] **前坂 俊之** (Abe Sada). Page 32.

[87] Ibid. Page 13.

[88] Ibid. Page 14.

[89] Ibid. Page 36.

[90] *Canadian Passenger Lists 1865-1935.* Library and Archives Canada. Ottawa, Ontario, Canada. Series RG76-C. Roll T-14909.

[91] "National Diet." Wikipedia.
https://en.wikipedia.org/wiki/National_Diet.

[92] Canadian Passenger Lists.

[93] **前坂 俊之** (Abe Sada). Pages 38-39.

[94] **Johnston, William.** *Geisha, Harlot, Strangler, Star.* Pages 182-184.

[95] **Schreiber Mark.** *The Dark Side: Infamous Japanese Crimes and Criminals.* "O-Sada Serves A Grateful Nation." Kodansha, 2001. Pages 184-190.

[96] **Johnston, William.** *Geisha, Harlot, Strangler, Star.* Pages 182-184.

[97] **前坂 俊之** (Abe Sada). "Jiken chosho zenbun". Page 44.

98 **Afshar, Dave.** "An Insider's Guide to Japan's Love Hotels." Culture Trip, 5 Mar. 2017. theculturetrip.com/asia/japan/articles/an-insiders-guide-to-japans-love-hotels/.

99 前坂 俊之 (Abe Sada). Pages 47-48.

100 前坂 俊之 (Abe Sada). Page 10.

101 前坂 俊之 (Abe Sada). Pages 49-57.

102 **Johnston, William.** *Geisha, Harlot, Strangler, Star.* Page 191.

103 "Japanese Cinema of the 1930's – Movie List." MUBI. mubi.com/lists/japanese-cinema-of-the-1930s.

104 **Johnston, William.** *Geisha, Harlot, Strangler, Star.* Page 194.

105 前坂 俊之 (Abe Sada). Page 64.

106 前坂 俊之 (Abe Sada). Page 122.

107 前坂 俊之 (Abe Sada). Page 83.

108 "Since Lancan: Papers of the Freudian School of Melbourne Vol.25," Chapter 19 --All The Way to Masaki Tea House. Clifton, Linda (ed.). Karnac Books, Ltd. 2016.

109 **Johnston, William.** *Geisha, Harlot, Strangler, Star.* Page 197.

110 Ibid.

111 U.S. Department of Health and Human services, National Institutes of Health, National Center for Advancing Translational Sciences. "Inxight: Drugs. BROMISOVAL." drugs.ncats.io/drug/469GW8R486.

112 **Johnston, William.** *Geisha, Harlot, Strangler, Star.* Page 199.

113 Ibid. Page 200.

114 **"Sada Abe."** Wikipedia. 27 Nov. 2018. https://en.wikipedia.org/wiki/Sada_Abe.

115 **Johnston, William.** *Geisha, Harlot, Strangler, Star.* Page 204.

116 **Schreiber, Mark.** *The Dark Side.*

117 **Johnston, William.** *Geisha, Harlot, Strangler, Star.* Page 201.

118 **Johnston, William.** *Geisha, Harlot, Strangler, Star.* Page 207.

119 **Schreiber, Mark.** *The Dark Side.*

120 "Shinagawa." Wikipedia. https://en.wikipedia.org/wiki/Shinagawa

121 **Conliffe, Ciaran.** "Abe Sada, Victim And Killer." Headstuff.Org. Oct. 3, 2016. www.Headstuff.Org/Culture/History/Abe-Sada-Victim-Killer/.

122 **Kingston, Jeff.** "1936 Coup Failed, but Rebels Killed Japan's 'Keynes'." The Japan Times, 2006. www.japantimes.co.jp/opinion/2016/02/20/commentary/1936-coup-failed-rebels-killed-japans-keynes/#.XFM_xc2IY2w.

123 **Schreiber, Mark.** *The Dark Side.*

124 **Kingston, Jeff.** *1936 Coup Failed.*

125 Ibid.

126 **Johnston, William.** *Geisha, Harlot, Strangler, Star.* Page 205.

[127] "1879: Takahashi Oden, Dokufu and She-Demon."ExecutedToday.com. ExecutedToday.com. www.executedtoday.com/2011/01/31/1879-dokufu-takahashi-oden-she-demon/.

[128] **Horinouchi, Masakazu.** 阿部定正伝 (*Abe Sada seiden*). Page 187.

[129] **Schreiber, Mark.** "With Amnesty or Death, Japan Seeks to Draw a Line under Heisei Era Crimes." The Japan Times, 17 Mar. 2018. www.japantimes.co.jp/news/2018/03/17/national/media-national/amnesty-death-japan-seeks-draw-line-heisei-era-crimes/#.XGcrrbiIY2w.

[130] **Schreiber Mark.** *The Dark Side.*

[131] **Horinouchi, Masakazu.** 阿部定正伝 (*Abe Sada seiden*). Page. 203.

[132] **Johnston, William.** *Geisha, Harlot, Strangler, Star.* Page 194

[133] **Horinouchi, Masakazu.** 阿部定正伝 (*Abe Sada seiden*). Page. 199.

[134] Ibid. Page 202.

[135] "Sada Abe." Wikipedia. Op. cit.

[136] **Johnston, William.** *Geisha, Harlot, Strangler, Star.* Page 124.

[137] Ibid. Page 136.

[138] **Horinouchi, Masakazu.** 阿部定正伝 (*Abe Sada seiden*). Page 239.

[139] "The Japanese Judicial System." Japan Federation of Bar Associations. https://www.nichibenren.or.jp/en/about/judicial_system/judicial_system.html.

[140] **Johnston, William.** *Geisha, Harlot, Strangler, Star.* Page 207.

[141] "Law of Japan." Wikipedia. https://en.wikipedia.org/wiki/Law_of_Japan.

[142] "An overview of the criminal law system in Japan." Government of Canada. https://travel.gc.ca/travelling/advisories/japan/criminal-law-system#criminal.

[143] "Criminal justice system of Japan." Wikipedia. https://en.wikipedia.org/wiki/Criminal_justice_system_of_Japan.

[144] "Judiciary of Germany." Wikipedia. https://en.wikipedia.org/wiki/Judiciary_of_Germany.

[145] **Johnston, William.** *Geisha, Harlot, Strangler, Star.* Page 125.

[146] Ibid. Page 131.

[147] **Vitelli, Romeo.** "The Abe Sada Incident (Part Two)." Providentia. July 31, 2016. https://drvitelli.typepad.com/providentia/2016/07/the-abe-sada-1.html

[148] Ibid.

[149] Schreiber, Mark. *The Dark Side.*

[150] Johnston, William. *Geisha, Harlot, Strangler, Star.* Page 140.

[151] Ibid. Page 158.

[152] Ibid. Page 139.

[153] Vitelli, Romeo. "The Abe Sada Incident (Part Two)."

[154] Johnston, William. *Geisha, Harlot, Strangler, Star.* Page 147.

[155] "Sakuradamon Incident (1932)." Wikipedia. https://en.wikipedia.org/wiki/Sakuradamon_Incident_ (1932).

[156] "Denma-Cho Prison." JAPAN THIS! 26 Sept. 2013. japanthis.com/2013/07/22/denma-cho-prison/.

[157] Schreiber, Mark. *The Dark Side.*

[158] Johnston, William. *Geisha, Harlot, Strangler, Star.* Page 142.

[159] Vitelli, Romeo. "The Abe Sada Incident (Part Two)."

[160] Conliffe, Ciaran. "Abe Sada, Victim and Killer."

[161] Sundberg, Steve. "2600th Anniversary of the Founding of Japan, 1940." Old Tokyo. www.oldtokyo.com/2600th-anniversary-of-the-founding-of-japan-1940/.

[162] Schreiber, Mark. "With Amnesty or Death."

[163] Johnston, William. *Geisha, Harlot, Strangler, Star.* Page 207.

[164] Schreiber, Mark. *The Dark Side.*

[165] Schreiber, Mark. Ibid.

[166] "Evacuations of civilians in Japan during World War II." Wikipedia. https://en.wikipedia.org/wiki/Evacuations_of_civilians_in_Japan_during_World_War_II.

[167] Johnston, William. *Geisha, Harlot, Strangler, Star.* Page 149.

[168] Kumazawa, J. and Yagisawa, M. "The history of antibiotics: The Japanese story." *Journal of Infection and Chemotherapy.* June 2002, Volume 8, Issue 2. Pages 125–133.

[169] Christensen, Kelly M. "Women's Suffrage in Japan in the 20th Century." Women's Suffrage and Beyond. January 5, 2012. http://womensuffrage.org/?p=389.

[170] Vitelli, Romeo. "The Abe Sada Incident (Part Two)."

[171] "Sada Abe." Wikipedia. Op. cit.

[172] Marran, Christine L. *Poison Woman: Figuring Female Transgression in Modern Japanese Culture.* University of Minnesota Press, 2007. Page 143.

[173] "Mikihiko Nagata." Wikipedia. https://en.wikipedia.org/wiki/Mikihiko_Nagata.

[174] Horinouchi, Masakazu. 阿部定正伝 (*Abe Sada seiden*). Page 297.

[175] Johnston, William. *Geisha, Harlot, Strangler, Star.* Page 152.

[176] Vitelli, Romeo. "The Abe Sada Incident (Part Two)."

[177] "Ero guro." Wikipedia. https://en.wikipedia.org/wiki/Ero_guro.

[178] "Buraiha." Wikipedia. https://en.wikipedia.org/wiki/Buraiha.

[179] **Marran, Christine L.** *Poison Woman.* Page 143.

[180] **Johnston, William.** *Geisha, Harlot, Strangler, Star.* Page 153.

[181] **Marran, Christine L.** *Poison Woman.* Page 143

[182] **Johnston, William.** *Geisha, Harlot, Strangler, Star.* Page 153.

[183] **Horinouchi, Masakazu.** 阿部定正伝 (*Abe Sada seiden*). Page 343.

[184] **Johnston, William.** *Geisha, Harlot, Strangler, Star.* Page 152.

[185] **Horinouchi, Masakazu.** 阿部定正伝 (*Abe Sada seiden*). Page 351.

[186] Ibid. Page 378.

[187] **Johnston, William.** *Geisha, Harlot, Strangler, Star.* Page 154.

[188] **Horinouchi, Masakazu.** 阿部定正伝 (*Abe Sada seiden*). Page 385.

[189] **Vitelli, Romeo.** "The Abe Sada Incident (Part Two)."

[190] **Johnston, William.** *Geisha, Harlot, Strangler, Star.* Page 207.

[191] "Ōkubo clan." Wikipedia. https://en.wikipedia.org/wiki/%C5%8Ckubo_clan.

[192] "Kazoku." Wikipedia. https://en.wikipedia.org/wiki/Kazoku.

[193] "1872: Yoarashi Okinu, Geisha." ExecutedToday.com. www.executedtoday.com/2011/03/28/1872-yoarashi-okinu-geisha/.

[194] **Marran, Christine L.** *Poison Woman.* Pages 79-86.

[195] "Noboru Tanaka." Wikipedia. https://en.wikipedia.org/wiki/Noboru_Tanaka.

[196] "A Woman Called Sada Abe." Wikipedia. https://en.wikipedia.org/wiki/A_Woman_Called_Sada_Abe.

[197] "Junko Miyashita." Wikipedia. https://en.wikipedia.org/wiki/Junko_Miyashita.

[198] **Kramer, Gary M.** "An Old, Obscene Genre Becomes a New Platform for Artistic Film." Salon. Salon.com. 3 July 2017. www.salon.com/2017/07/03/roman-porno-reboot-project/.

[199] "Censorship in Japan." Wikipedia. https://en.wikipedia.org/wiki/Censorship_in_Japan.

[200] "Inejiro Asanuma." Wikipedia. https://en.wikipedia.org/wiki/Inejiro_Asanuma.

[201] "Nagisa Oshima." Wikipedia. https://en.wikipedia.org/wiki/Nagisa_Oshima.

[202] "Sada Abe." Wikipedia. Op. cit.

[203] "Meiji · Taishô · Shôwa: Ryôki Onna Hanzai-Shi." IMDb, IMDb.com, www.imdb.com/title/tt0142652/.

[204] "Teruo Ishii." Wikipedia. https://en.wikipedia.org/wiki/Teruo_Ishii.

[205] "Meiji · Taishô · Shôwa: Ryôki Onna Hanzai-Shi." Op.cit.

[206] *Original Body Kingdom/Gala Abe Sada 1936.* Wikipedia, Wikimedia Foundation, 5 Nov. 2018. en.wikipedia.org/wiki/Original_Body_Kingdom_/_Gala_Abe_Sada_1936#Track_listing.

[207] **Schreiber, Mark.** *The Dark Side.*

[208] **Molony, Barbara.** "Feminism in Japan." Asian History. Oxford Research Encyclopedias. January 2018. http://oxfordre.com/asianhistory/view/10.1093/acrefore/9780190 277727.001.0001/acrefore-9780190277727-e-194.

[209] "Kishida Toshiko (1863–1901)." Women in World History: A Biographical Encyclopedia. 2002. Encyclopedia.com. https://www.encyclopedia.com/women/encyclopedias-almanacs-transcripts-and-maps/kishida-toshiko-1863-1901.

[210] "Toshiko Kishida." Wikipedia. https://en.wikipedia.org/wiki/Toshiko_Kishida.

[211] "Fukuda Hideko." Wikipedia. https://en.wikipedia.org/wiki/Fukuda_Hideko.

[212] **Molony, Barbara.** Op. cit.

[213] **Adelstein, Jake.** "Equal-opportunity infidelity comes to Japan." The Japan Times. July 6, 2013. https://www.japantimes.co.jp/news/2013/07/06/national/media-national/equal-opportunity-infidelity-comes-to-japan/#.XK4pUaRlA2w.

[214] Ibid.

[215] **Yoshida, Reiji.** "Banning women from the sumo ring: centuries-old tradition, straight-up sexism or something more complex?" TheJapanTimes. April 30, 2018. https://www.japantimes.co.jp/news/2018/04/30/national/social-issues/banning-women-sumo-ring-sexism-centuries-old-cultural-tradition/#.XMnbdaRlA2w.

[216] **Motoko, Rich.** "As a New Emperor Is Enthroned in Japan, His Wife Won't Be Allowed to Watch." The New York Times. April 29, 2019. https://www.nytimes.com/2019/04/29/world/asia/japan-emperor-women.html?Fbclid=IwAR0UpD_D5zZIQ21WtygIrvYDenuC3CF332S1K0QvylLts8ZpDNHaU0AOc6U.

[217] **Yamaguchi, Mari.** "Japanese Medical School Confirms Altering Test Scores to Limit Women."- The Boston Globe. BostonGlobe.com, 7 Aug. 2018. www.bostonglobe.com/news/world/2018/08/07/japanese-medical-school-confirms-altering-test-scores-limit-women/Rl1SN7H3kOdkMACWVPTPYI/story.html.

[218] **Johnston, William.** *Geisha, Harlot, Strangler, Star.* Page 141.

[219] "Kyoto 'black widow' faces third arrest for Kobe poisoning." Tokyo Reporter. June 11, 2015. https://www.tokyoreporter.com/japan/kyoto/kyoto-black-widow-faces-third-arrest-for-kobe-poisoning/.

[220] **Reddy, Sujata.** "How 71-yr-old serial killer, Chisako Kakehi, baited and preyed on old, lonely & wealthy men." The Economic Times. November 23, 2017. https://economictimes.indiatimes.com/magazines/panache/how-71-yr-old-serial-killer-chisako-kakehi-baited-and-preyed-on-old-lonely-wealthy-men/articleshow/61762915.cms?from=mdr.

[221] **Sim, Walter.** "How Japan's Black Widow baited and killed her prey." The Straits Times, Nov 13, 2017. https://www.straitstimes.com/asia/east-asia/how-japans-black-widow-baited-and-killed-her-prey.

[222] "Chisako Kakehi." Wikipedia. https://en.wikipedia.org/wiki/Chisako_Kakehi.

[223] **Schmidt, Samantha.** "Japan's 'black widow' sentenced to hang for killing husbands, lovers with cyanide." The Washington Post, November 7, 2017. https://www.washingtonpost.com/news/morning-mix/wp/2017/11/07/japans-black-widow-sentenced-to-hang-for-killing-husbands-lovers-with-cyanide/?utm_term=.78781745a111.

[224] "Obsessive Jealousy." Institut Psicològic Internacional. https://www.ipitia.com/obsessive-jealousy/.

[225] "Overadaptation." Behavenet. Behavenet.com/overadaptation.

[226] "Obsessive Jealousy." Op. cit.

List of Illustrations

List of Photographs

History Vol. 7, published by Mainichi Newspapers Company. Public domain via Wikimedia Commons.

Bibliography

"1872: Yoarashi Okinu, Geisha." ExecutedToday.com. Accessed March 21, 2019. www.executedtoday.com/2011/03/28/1872-yoarashi-okinu-geisha/.

"1879: Takahashi Oden, dokufu and she-demon." ExecutedToday.com. Accessed February 19, 2019. www.executedtoday.com/2011/01/31/1879-dokufu-takahashi-oden-she-demon/.

"A Woman Called Sada Abe." Wikipedia. Accessed February 15, 2019. https://en.wikipedia.org/wiki/A_Woman_Called_Sada_Abe.

前坂 俊之. (Abe Sada) 阿部定手記—愛の半生 (*Abe sada shuki – ai no hansei* (*Memoirs of Sada Abe*). Chuokoron-sha, Inc., 1948.

Abe Sada. *Jiken chosho zenbun: Inochi kezuru seiai no onna (Japanese Edition)*. [Police Investigation Report- Full Text]. Kosumikku Intanashonaru. January 1, 1997.

"Abe Sada Incident (Part Two), The." typepad.com/Providentia. July 31, 2016. Accessed February 2, 2019. https://drvitelli.typepad.com/providentia/2016/07/the-abe-sada-1.html.

Adelstein, Jake. "Equal-opportunity infidelity comes to Japan." The Japan Times. July 6, 2013. Accessed April 10, 2019. https://www.japantimes.co.jp/news/2013/07/06/national/media-national/equal-opportunity-infidelity-comes-to-japan/#.XK4pUaRlA2w.

Afshar, Dave. "An Insider's Guide to Japan's Love Hotels." Culture Trip, 5 Mar. 2017. Accessed February 13, 2019. theculturetrip.com/asia/japan/articles/an-insiders-guide-to-japans-love-hotels/.

"An overview of the criminal law system in Japan." Government of Canada. Accessed March 25, 2019.

https://travel.gc.ca/travelling/advisories/japan/criminal-law-system#criminal.

Anderson, Patricia. "Roles of Samurai Women: Social Norms and Inner Conflicts During Japan's Tokugawa Period, 1603-1868." *New Views on Gender –Volume 15*. February, 2015.

"Arsphenamine." Wikipedia. Accessed February 28, 2019. https://en.wikipedia.org/wiki/Arsphenamine.

"Asakusa: The Heart of Old Tokyo." JAPANISTRY. 6 Aug. 2018. Accessed February 7, 2019. www.japanistry.com/asakusa//.

Boskey, Elizabeth and Olender, Susan. "Is It Possible to Get the Same STD Twice?" Verywell Health. Accessed February 28, 2019. www.verywellhealth.com/can-i-get-the-same-std-a-second-time-3133003.

"Buraiha." Wikipedia. Accessed April 1, 2019. https://en.wikipedia.org/wiki/Buraiha.

Canadian Passenger Lists, 1865-1935. Library and Archives Canada. Ottawa, Ontario, Canada. Series RG76-C. Roll T-14909.

"Censorship in Japan." Wikipedia. Accessed February 22, 2019. https://en.wikipedia.org/wiki/Censorship_in_Japan.

"Chisako Kakehi." Wikipedia. Accessed April 4, 2019. https://en.wikipedia.org/wiki/Chisako_Kakehi.

Christensen, Kelly M. "Women's Suffrage in Japan in the 20th Century." *Women's Suffrage and Beyond*. January 5, 2012. Accessed April 2, 2019. http://womensuffrage.org/?p=389.

Cichocki, Mark and Olender, Susan. "Get Familiar With the Symptoms of Syphilis." Verywell Health. Accessed February 28, 2019. www.verywellhealth.com/syphilis-signs-and-symptoms-49530.

Conliffe, Ciaran. "Abe Sada, Victim And Killer." HeadStuff. Oct. 3, 2016. Accessed February 4, 2019. www.head-stuff.org/culture/history/abe-sada-victim-killer/.

"Criminal justice system of Japan." Wikipedia. Accessed Marc 25, 2019. https://en.wikipedia.org/wiki/Criminal_justice_system_of_Japan.

"Denkikan." Wikipedia. Accessed February 11, 1019. www.en.m.wikipedia.org/wiki/Denkikan.

"Denma-Cho Prison." JAPAN THIS! 26 Sept. 2013. Accessed March 29, 2019. japanthis.com/2013/07/22/denma-cho-prison/.

Dias, Maria Suzette Fernandes. *Legacies of Slavery: Comparative Perspectives*. Cambridge Scholars Publishing, 2007.

"Ero guro." Wikipedia. Accessed February 15, 2019. https://en.wikipedia.org/wiki/Ero_guro.

"Evacuations of civilians in Japan during World War II." Wikipedia. Accessed April 1, 2019. https://en.wikipedia.org/wiki/Evacuations_of_civilians_in_Japan_during_World_War_II.

"Fukuda Hideko." Wikipedia. Accessed April 9, 2019. https://en.wikipedia.org/wiki/Fukuda_Hideko.

Greve, Gabi. "Dokufu Poisonous Woman." Dokufu Poisonous Woman, 2 June 2016. Accessed March 22, 2019. edoflourishing.blogspot.com/2016/06/dokufu-poisonous-woman.html.

Hoffman, Michael. "The rarely, if ever, told story of Japanese sold as slaves by Portuguese traders." The Japan Times. May 26, 2013.

Horinouchi, Masakazu. 阿部定正伝 （Abe Sada seiden）. 東京: 情報センター出版局, 1998.

"Inejiro Asanuma." Wikipedia. Accessed April 4, 2019. https://en.wikipedia.org/wiki/Inejiro_Asanuma.

"Infanticide in Japan: Sign of the Times?" The New York Times. December 8, 1973.

Ishimaru, Yasko. "Omiai." Johns Hopkins University. September 2003. Accessed January 29, 2019. faculty.tru.ca/jhu/Omiai.pdf.

"Japanese Cinema of the 1930's – Movie List." MUBI. Accessed March 1, 2019. mubi.com/lists/japanese-cinema-of-the-1930s.

"Japanese Judicial System, The." Japan Federation of Bar Associations. Accessed March 25, 2019. https://www.nichibenren.or.jp/en/about/judicial_system/judicial_system.html.

"Japanese Medical School Confirms Altering Test Scores to Limit Women - The Boston Globe." BostonGlobe.com, 7 Aug. 2018, Accessed March 22, 2019. www.bostonglobe.com/news/world/ 2018/08/07/japanese-medical-school-confirms-altering-test-scores-limit-women/Rl1SN7H3kOdkMACWVPTPYI/story.html.

Johnston, Eric. "Love Town Where Time Stands Still." The Japan Times, July 8, 2001.

Johnston, William. *Geisha, Harlot, Strangler, Star: A Woman, Sex, and Moral Values in Modern Japan.* Columbia University Press, 2005.

"Judiciary of Germany." Wikipedia. Accessed March 26, 2019. https://en.wikipedia.org/wiki/Judiciary_of_Germany.

"Junko Miyashita." Wikipedia. Accessed April 4, 2019. https://en.wikipedia.org/wiki/Junko_Miyashita.

"Kanda, Tokyo." Wikipedia. Accessed February 4, 2019. https://en.wikipedia.org/wiki/Kanda,_Tokyo.

Kapur, Roshni. "Welcome to the Family: Adult Adoptions in Corporate Japan." Rappler, 2016. Accessed February 6, 2019. www.rappler.com/world/regions/asia-pa-cific/119305-japan-adult-male-adoption.

"Kazoku." Wikipedia. Accessed April 2, 2019. https://en.wikipedia.org/wiki/Kazoku.

Kingston, Jeff. "1936 coup failed, but rebels killed Japan's 'Keynes'." The Japan Times: Commentary/Counterpoint. Accessed January 31, 2019. https://www.japan-times.co.jp/opinion/2016/02/20/commentary/1936-coup-failed-rebels-killed-japans-keynes/#.XFM_xc2IY2w.

"Kishida Toshiko (1863–1901)." Women in World History: A Biographical Encyclopedia. 2002. Encyclopedia.com. Accessed April 10, 2019. https://www.encyclope-dia.com/women/encyclopedias-almanacs-transcripts-and-maps/kishida-toshiko-1863-1901.

Kramer, Gary M. "An Old, Obscene Genre Becomes a New Platform for Artistic Film." Salon.com, 3 July 2017. Accessed February 15, 2019. www.sa-lon.com/2017/07/03/roman-porno-reboot-project/.

Kumazawa, J. and Yagisawa, M. "The history of antibiotics: The Japanese story." *Journal of Infection and Chemotherapy*. June 2002, Volume 8, Issue 2, pp 125–133.

"Kyoto 'black widow' faces third arrest for Kobe poisoning." Tokyo Reporter. June 11, 2015. Accessed April 10, 2019. https://www.tokyoreporter.com/japan/kyoto/kyoto-black-widow-faces-third-arrest-for-kobe-poisoning/.

"Law of Japan." Wikipedia. Accessed March 25, 2019. https://en.wikipedia.org/wiki/Law_of_Japan.

Linhard, Sepp and Fruhstuck, Sabine (ed.). *The Culture of Japan as Seen Through Its Leisure*. State University of New York Press. 1998.

Marran, Christine L. *Poison Woman: Figuring Female Transgression in Modern Japanese Culture.* University of Minnesota Press, 2007.

"Meiji · Taishô · Shôwa: Ryôki Onna Hanzai-Shi." IMDb, IMDb.com. Accessed February 19, 2019. www.imdb.com/title/tt0142652/.

"Mikihiko Nagata." Wikipedia. Accessed April 1, 2019. https://en.wikipedia.org/wiki/Mikihiko_Nagata.

Molony, Barbara. "Feminism in Japan." Asian History. Oxford Research Encyclopedias. January 2018. Accessed April 9, 2019. http://oxfordre.com/asianhistory/view/10.1093/acrefore/9780190277727.001.0001/acrefore-9780190277727-e-194.

Monumenta Nipponica: Studies on Japanese Culture, Past and Present, Volume 59, Issues 3-4. Sophia University, 2004.

Moran, J. F. *The Japanese and the Jesuits: Alessandro Valignano in Sixteenth Century Japan,* 1st Edition. Routledge, 1993.

Motoko, Rich. "As a New Emperor Is Enthroned in Japan, His Wife Won't Be Allowed to Watch." The New York Times. April 29, 2019. Accessed May 1, 2019. https://www.nytimes.com/2019/04/29/ world/asia/japan-emperor-women.html?Fbclid=IwAR0UpD_D5zZIQ21WtygIrvYDenuC3CF332S1K0QvylLts8ZpDNHaU0AOc6U.

"Nagisa Oshima." Wikipedia. Accessed February 22, 2019. https://en.wikipedia.org/wiki/Nagisa_Oshima.

Narayan, S. "Women in Meiji Japan: Exploring the Underclass of Japanese Industrialization." *Inquiries Journal/Student Pulse.* Accessed January 24, 2019. http://www.inquiriesjournal.com/articles/1369/women-in-meiji-japan-exploring-the-underclass-of-japanese-industrialization.

"National Diet." Wikipedia. Accessed March 1, 2019. https://en.wikipedia.org/wiki/National_Diet.

"Noboru Tanaka." Wikipedia. Accessed February 22, 2019. https://en.wikipedia.org/wiki/Noboru_Tanaka.

Norgren, Tiana. *Abortion before Birth Control: The Politics of Reproduction in Postwar Japan*. Princeton University Press, 2001.

"Obsessive Jealousy." Institut Psicològic Internacional. Accessed April 16, 2019. https://www.ipitia.com/obsessive-jealousy/.

"Okubo clan." Wikipedia. Accessed April 2, 2019. https://en.wikipedia.org/wiki/%C5%8Ckubo_clan.

"Original Body Kingdom / Gala Abe Sada 1936." Wikipedia, Wikimedia Foundation, 5 Nov. 2018. Accessed February 19, 2019. en.wikipedia.org/wiki/Original_Body_Kingdom_/_Gala_Abe_Sada_1936#Track_listing.

"Overadaptation." Behavenet. Accessed April 17, 2019. Behavenet.com/overadaptation.

"Perry Expedition." Wikipedia. Accessed March 7, 2019. https://en.wikipedia.org/wiki/Perry_Expedition.

"Prostitute Emancipation Act." Samurai-Archives, 2014. Accessed February 26, 2019. wiki.samurai-archives.com/index.php?title=Prostitute_Emancipation_Act.

Ravina, Mark. *The Last Samurai: The Life and Battles of Saigo Takamori*. John Wiley & Sons, 2011.

Reddy, Sujata. "How 71-yr-old serial killer, Chisako Kakehi, baited and preyed on old, lonely & wealthy men." The Economic Times. November 23, 2017. Accessed April 10, 2019. https://economictimes.indiatimes.com/magazines/panache/how-71-yr-old-serial-killer-chisako-kakehi-baited-and-preyed-on-old-lonely-wealthy-men/articleshow/61762915.cms?from=mdr.

"Rikken Seiyikai." Wikipedia. Accessed March 13, 2019. https://en.wikipedia.org/wiki/Rikken_Seiy%C5%ABkai.

Robins-Mowry, Dorothy. *The Hidden Sun: Women of Modern Japan*. Westview Press, 1983.

"Sada Abe." Wikipedia. Accessed January 25, 2019. https://en.wikipedia.org/wiki/Sada_Abe.

"Sakuradamon Incident (1932)." Wikipedia. https://en.wikipedia.org/wiki/Sakuradamon_Incident_ (1932).

Sanderson, Beck. *Ethics of Civilization (Volume 21) East Asia 1800-1949*. World Peace Communications, 2007. Accessed January 25, 2019. http://www.san.beck.org/21-7-JapanModernization1800-94.html.

Schmidt, Samantha. "Japan's 'black widow' sentenced to hang for killing husbands, lovers with cyanide." The Washington Post, November 7, 2017. Accessed April 4, 2019. https://www.washingtonpost.com/news/morning-mix/wp/2017/11/07/japans-black-widow-sentenced-to-hang-for-killing-husbands-lovers-with-cyanide/?utm_term=.78781745a111.

Schreiber Mark. *The Dark Side: Infamous Japanese Crimes and Criminals*. "O-Sada Serves A Grateful Nation." Kodansha, 2001.

Schreiber, Mark. "With Amnesty or Death, Japan Seeks to Draw a Line under Heisei Era Crimes." The Japan Times, 17 Mar. 2018.

"Shinagawa." Wikipedia. Accessed February 13, 2019. https://en.wikipedia.org/wiki/Shinagawa.

Sim, Walter. "How Japan's Black Widow baited and killed her prey." The Straits Times. Nov 13, 2017. Accessed April 4, 2019. https://www.straitstimes.com/asia/east-asia/how-japans-black-widow-baited-and-killed-her-prey.

Stephenson, Andrea Lind. "Culture of Desire: The History and Development of Sexual Services in Japan." Skemman, 7 May 2018. Accessed February 6, 2019. skemman.is/handle/1946/30004.

Sundberg, Steve. "2600th Anniversary of the Founding of Japan, 1940." Old Tokyo. Accessed February 15, 2019. www.oldtokyo.com/2600th-anniversary-of-the-founding-of-japan-1940/.

Szczepanski, Kallie. "The Four-Tiered Class System of Feudal Japan." Thought Co. April 22, 2018. Accessed February 25, 2019. https://www.thoughtco.com/four-tiered-class-system-feudal-japan-195582.

"Taikomochi - the Male Geisha." h2g2 The Hitchhiker's Guide to the Galaxy: Earth Edition (June 23, 2014). Accessed February 11, 2019. h2g2.com/edited_entry/A87805623.

"Teruo Ishii." Wikipedia. Accessed February 22, 2019. https://en.wikipedia.org/wiki/Teruo_Ishii.

"THE TAKARAZUKA REVUE'S ALLURE." TAKARAZUKA REVUE Official Website. Accessed March 13, 2019. kageki.hankyu.co.jp/English/about/index.html.

"Tobita Shinchi." Wikipedia. Accessed January 31, 2019. https://en.wikipedia.org/wiki/Tobita_Shinchi.

"Tokyo-Yokohama Earthquake of 1923." Encyclopædia Britannica. 25 Aug. 2018. Accessed February 4, 2019. www.britannica.com/event/Tokyo-Yokohama-earthquake-of-1923.

Tull, Matthew, and Steven Gans. "Symptoms of PTSD After a Rape." Verywell Mind, Dotdash, Accessed February 27, 2019. www.verywellmind.com/symptoms-of-ptsd-after-a-rape-2797203.

"Toshiko Kishida." Wikipedia. Accessed April 9, 2019. https://en.wikipedia.org/wiki/Toshiko_Kishida.

U.S. Department of Health and Human services, National Institutes of Health, National Center for Advancing Translational Sciences. "NCATS Inxight: Drugs - BROMISOVAL." Inxight Drugs. Accessed February 13, 2019. drugs.ncats.io/drug/469GW8R486.

Weiner, Michael. Ed. *Race, Ethnicity and Migration in Modern Japan: Imagined and imaginary minorities.* Taylor & Francis, 2004.

What Is Dotonbori?" Official Web Site The Shopping District of Dotonbori. Accessed March 12, 2019. www.dotonbori.or.jp/en/about/index.html.

Yamamoto, Marie and Adelstein, Jake. "Does Japan Ever Convict Men for Rape?" The Daily Beast. 11 May 2017. Accessed February 8, 2019. www.thedailybeast.com/does-japan-ever-convict-men-for-rape.

"Yamanote and Shitamachi." Wikipedia. Accessed February 4, 2019. en.wikipedia.org/wiki/Yamanote_and_Shitamachi.

"Yoarashi Okinu." Wikipedia. Accessed March 21, 2019. https://en.wikipedia.org/wiki/Yoarashi_Okinu.

Yoshida, Reiji. "Banning women from the sumo ring: centuries-old tradition, straight-up sexism or something more complex?" TheJapanTimes. April 30, 2018. Accessed May 1, 2019. https://www.japantimes.co.jp/news/2018/04/30/national/social-issues/banning-women-sumo-ring-sexism-centuries-old-cultural-tradition/#.XMnbdaRlA2w.

Index

ABOUT THE AUTHOR

KRISTINE OHKUBO IS an avid traveler, blogger, and Japanophile. A graduate of DePaul University, she developed a deep love and appreciation of Japanese culture, people, and history early in life. Her travels in Japan have enabled her to gain insight into this fascinating culture, which she shares with you through her work.

Her first book, a travel guide to Japan, was published in 2016. In 2017, she released a historical study of the Pacific War written from the perspective of the Japanese people, both those who were living in Japan and in the United States, when the war broke out. She supplemented her releases in 2019 with a work that examines the influences of Western culture and Freemasonry on the Westernization and subsequent modernization of China and Japan.

Kristine's latest book tells the story of an infamous twentieth century geisha who was both a victim and an aggressor, struggling amidst a strict patriarchal culture and a rapidly changing social system.

Kristine believes that writing from other cultural perspectives encourages empathy and understanding, and at the same time broadens our knowledge of the events which have unfolded over the years.

As an author, she encourages her readers to let their curiosity and hunger for knowledge be boundless, as she invites them to explore her work.

PLEASE TURN THE PAGE FOR AN EXCERPT FROM:

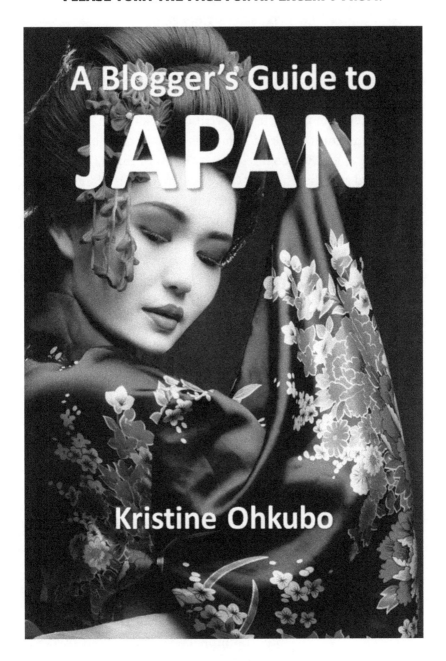

ISBN-13: 978-1539033110

Taito-ku (台東区): Taito Ward
Asakusa District (浅草)

Located in Tokyo's Taito Ward, Asakusa was once considered the leading entertainment district. Today it is a notable tourist attraction known for its many temples and a place where one can get a genuine sense of what old Tokyo was like.

The 7th century Sensoji Temple is most popular of Asakusa's temples and easily recognized by its Furai Jin-mon (Gate of the Wind God and the Thunder God), adorned with a large red paper lantern that bears the inscription "Kaminari-mon (Thunder Gate)." The temple enjoys a constant flow of visitors and worshippers throughout the year.

Upon approaching the temple, tourists encounter a centuries-old shopping street known as Nakamise, where you can purchase traditional souvenirs and snacks from the local region. Next to the temple grounds is a small amusement park called Hanayashiki, which originally opened as a flower park in 1853 and is the oldest amusement park in Japan.

Aside from Sensoji Temple, visitors to Asakusa can enjoy a cruise down the Sumida River, which departs from a wharf located within a five-minute walk from the temple. Tokyo Skytree is only a 20-minute walk across the Sumida River from Asakusa.

Although it is relatively easy to get around Asakusa on foot, you may consider taking a guided tour of the area in one of the many rickshaws available. A 30-minute tour generally costs around ¥8,000.

An interesting fact about Asakusa is that the area was heavily damaged by U.S. bombing raids during World War II, particularly the March 1945 firebombing of Tokyo. Consequently, there are very few buildings dating back to the pre-1950s. However, one can still find traditional ryokans (guest-houses), homes, and small-scale apartment buildings scattered throughout the district.

With so many religious establishments, there are frequent matsuri (Shinto festivals) in Asakusa, as each temple or shrine hosts at least one matsuri a year, if not every season. The largest and most popular is the Sanja Matsuri in May, when roads are closed from dawn until late evening.

The district is also famous for its senbei (rice crackers), grilled on the spot, flavored with soy and usually wrapped in seaweed. There are many competing shops in the Nakamise arcade serving these delicious treats and the Japanese locals typically purchase packages of senbei as souvenirs for family and friends.

Regardless of what draws you to Asakusa, the district remains one of Tokyo's top destinations for foreigners and locals alike.

Location(s): Taito-ku, Tokyo
Web Page: http://asakusa-nakamise.jp/e-index.html

Taito-ku (台東区): Taito Ward
Asakusa (浅草) District: Samba Carnival

Every year since 1981, together with samba teams from Brazil, about 4,700 lovers of samba dancing from all over Japan converge on Asakusa the last Saturday in August for what is known as one of the largest events in Tokyo. As a town that grew up around a temple, Asakusa observes many traditional festivals, but the Samba Carnival is a relatively new event. It started when the Mayor of Taito invited the winning group from that year's Rio Carnival to put on a display. The dance trend quickly caught on and samba became a part of Asakusa's rich tradition. As a matter of fact, the district is full of tributes to Brazilian culture and customs, including several of Japan's most popular samba schools.

During this one day event, 30 to 40 teams compete for prizes. The largest of these teams consist of 250 performers. The competition is usually broken into three tiers of dancers classified by their skill level and commitment to the highly technical art of samba dancing. The top league is comprised of dancers who are seriously committed to dancing, those who put on original dances with a high degree of technical skill, and musicians who can expertly play South American percussion instruments. The participants in leagues 2 and 3 are basically there to enjoy dancing the samba and participating in the costume parade.

The event characterized by its gorgeous costumes, intricate floats, and a healthy dose of sultry samba dancing draws more than 500,000 visitors annually. Considerable effort is put into making the costumes and floats. Colorful plumes and thousands of sequins are combined with an enormous amount of originality and creativity to produce fabulous outfits, some of which are so big you can hardly see the performers wearing them! Some teams try to achieve a glamorous spectacle while others go for the funny and ridiculous. Each group is accompanied by its own band, in which drums and Latin-American percussion instruments dominate. Most of the performers are young women, but there are kids, men, and older performers too. Every year, the winning team from the Rio Carnival is invited to Asakusa and they parade alongside the local teams.

A prize is awarded to the best team as determined by the judges and another based on mobile-phone voting by the general public. There are also extra prizes awarded by carnival sponsors. Although the parade is limited to Kaminarimon-dori and Umamichi-dori near Sensoji Temple, there is an overwhelming atmosphere of energy and exuberance throughout Asakusa on the day of the event.

To reach the event, use the Ginza or Toei Asakusa Subway Line exiting at Asakusa Station. Admission to the carnival is free.

Location(s): Taito-ku, Tokyo
Web Page: http://www.asakusa-samba.org/

PLEASE TURN THE PAGE FOR AN EXCERPT FROM:

ISBN-13: 978-1540747952

THE ALLIED OCCUPATION OF JAPAN

When Emperor Hirohito announced Japan's unconditional surrender on the radio on August 15, 1945, it was his first radio broadcast and the first time the majority of Japanese citizens actually heard his voice. This date became known as V-J Day or Victory over Japan Day in America. The same name was given to September 2, 1945, when the Japanese officially signed the surrender document aboard the battleship USS Missouri. In Japan, however, August 15 was known as Shusen Kinenbi (Memorial Day for the End of the War). This name was officially changed in 1982 by an ordinance adopted by the Japanese government, and today August 15 is known as Senbotsusha o Tsuitoshi Heiwa o Kinensuru Hi (Day For Mourning of War Dead and Praying for Peace).

On August 28, 150 United States personnel arrived at Atsugi City in Kanagawa prefecture. The Atsugi Kaigun Hikojo (the Naval Air Facility Atsugi) is located just 7.4 km (4.6 miles) east-northeast of the city, and it is the largest United States naval air base in the Pacific Ocean today. The United States shares the base with the Japan Maritime Self-Defense Force.

The base was originally constructed in 1938 by the Imperial Japanese Navy and was home to the Japanese 302 Naval Aviation Corps, one of Japan's most formidable fighter squadrons during World War II. It is documented that aircraft based at Atsugi Kaigun Hikojo managed to shoot down over 300 American bombers during the fire bombings of 1945. Following Japan's surrender, many of the Japanese pilots stationed at the base refused to follow the emperor's orders to lay down their arms. Instead, they took to the skies and dropped countless leaflets over the cities of Tokyo and Yokohama, urging locals to resist the American forces. Eventually, these pilots gave up and abandoned Atsugi.

General Douglas MacArthur, appointed as the Supreme Commander of the Allied Forces, arrived in Tokyo on August

30. Although Great Britain, the Soviet Union, and the Republic of China had an advisory role as part of the Allied Council, MacArthur had the final authority to make all decisions. Shortly after his arrival, several laws were put into place. Allied personnel were forbidden to assault the Japanese people or to eat their scarce food. Japanese people were forbidden to fly the Hinomaru, or Rising Sun flag, until 1948, when the restriction was partially lifted. It was fully lifted a year later.

Despite these laws, the US troops committed countless rapes throughout Japan, many of which went unreported.

Following the Battle of Okinawa, thousands of rapes occurred on the Ryukyu Islands. There were 76 cases of rape or rape-murder reported in Okinawa alone during the first five years of occupation.

But perhaps the most disturbing of these cases took place ten years into the United States occupation of Okinawa. The case, referred to as the Yumiko Nagayama Incident, involved the rape and murder of a six-year-old child by a 31-year-old American soldier named Isaac J. Hurt. Sergeant Hurt was a member of B Battalion, 32nd Artillery Division and stationed in Okinawa. The little girl was reported missing on September 3, 1955 and her mutilated body was discovered in a garbage dump at Kadena Air Base the next day.

Sergeant Hurt was brought up on rape and murder charges by a United States court-martial, convicted, and sentenced to death. However, his case was later appealed. He was returned to the United States and was set free. At the time, he was the second United States serviceman convicted of rape in Okinawa in less than one month.

The sexual crimes committed in Okinawa prompted the Japanese authorities to set up a system of prostitution facilities known as the Recreation and Amusement Association (RAA) to protect the Japanese women living on the mainland. The organization was created on August 28 and was initially referred to as the "Special Comfort Facilities Association."

By the end of 1945, more than 350,000 United States personnel were stationed throughout Japan. The Japanese strategy was to utilize "experienced women" to protect the average women and girls from harm. They established 34 facilities, 16 of which were actually used for prostitution. At its peak, the RAA had 20,000 prostitutes working for the organization.

But where did the RAA get 20,000 "experienced women?" It was a well-known fact that the Japanese government had cracked down on prostitution in Tokyo, prompting many women in the trade to flee the city. Also, the famous Yoshiwara red light district only had 2,000 prostitutes prior to the war and that number dwindled down to only a few dozen by the war's end.

Therefore, the RAA recruited widely from the general population, using carefully worded advertisements posted in front of their offices and in newspapers. These ads emphasized generous work conditions, which included free accommodation, meals, and clothes, and avoided providing the actual details concerning the nature of the work. Most women left upon learning of the deception, but some stayed.

Many of those that did stay did so due to the desperate financial situation of their families. There were widespread poverty and food shortages at the time. Many of the women were urged by their parents to become prostitutes or possessed a willingness to sacrifice themselves to help their families. The RAA also took advantage of the large number of orphaned and widowed young women.

In addition to the prostitutes, the RAA also recruited a large number of "dancers" who were paid to dance with soldiers. However, over time, the distinction between "dancer" and "prostitute" became blurred.

Faced with the unprecedented rise in venereal disease among the American soldiers, MacArthur closed down the prostitution facilities on March 27, 1946, after which time the incidence of rape increased significantly. When the RAA was in existence, it was estimated that the number of rapes and as-saults on Japanese women averaged 40 incidences per day. Af-ter the closure of the facilities, that number increased to an average of 330 incidences per day. The sexual and violent crimes were most prevalent in naval ports, such as Yokohama and Yokosuka. Two weeks into the occupation, the Occupation Administration began censoring all media, including any men-tion of rape or other sensitive social issues. However, this did not completely prevent the local newspapers from leaking in-formation from time to time. One example was the local news-paper, Daily Ise Shimbun, which was suspended for twenty-four hours on December 27, 1945, for violating the Allied Press Code.

The closing of the RAA also saw the rise of what became known as "pan-pan girls." The term was a derogatory one and used to describe prostitutes who walked the streets. Many women who worked for the RAA suddenly found themselves out of work when the organization closed its doors. Conse-quently, they took to the streets and became private and illegal prostitutes. The pan-pan girls dressed in Western attire and so-licited around bars, public transport stations, and on the street. They were often seen walking down the street holding on to the arms of tall, uniformed American GIs. These women soon be-came the symbols of the Allied Occupation of Japan.

PLEASE TURN THE PAGE FOR AN EXCERPT FROM:

KRISTINE OHKUBO

ASIA'S MASONIC REFORMATION

FREEMASONRY'S IMPACT ON THE
WESTERNIZATION AND SUBSEQUENT
MODERNIZATION OF ASIA

ISBN-13: 978-1727377316

BUSHIDO, SHINTO, FREEMASONRY

Upon examining Japan's evolution from a closed country to a free-trading, modern nation, it becomes apparent that the traders, many of whom were associated with Freemasonry, played a crucial role. One trader in particular was highly instrumental in helping to cast off the age of feudalism and usher in the modern age. His name was Thomas Blake Glover.

Thomas Glover was a Scottish trader who provided arms and assistance to the anti-Tokugawa Choshu clan through his Nagasaki-based trading company. Sakamoto Ryoma, a prominent figure in the movement to overthrow the Tokugawa Shogunate and a close friend of Glover's, purchased arms with funds provided by the Satsuma clan for the venture. Ryoma had fled to Kagoshima in the Satsuma domain in 1864, a time when Kagoshima was developing as a major center for the anti-Tokugawa movement.

Sakamoto Ryoma was born in central Kochi, which in feudal times was known as the Tosa domain, on January 3, 1836, to a successful merchant and his wife. Although his father was only a lower-class merchant, his success enabled him to purchase the right to be a lower-ranked samurai. At the time, there were four distinct social classes in Japan: samurai, farmer, artisan, and merchant.

He began his studies in kendo at age 14 and became a very skillful swordsman. After completing his studies in 1853, he was sent to Edo (Tokyo) to further develop his technique. In time, he acquired the reputation as one of the most accomplished masters of the sword among the students who had been sent to Edo by their clans. The dominant clans at the time were: Satsuma, Choshu, and Tosa.

When Admiral Perry arrived in Edo Bay with his famous black ships in 1853, the Shogun ordered the daimyo of these clans to guard Edo Bay. The students from Tosa were gathered to carry out the order and Ryoma was among them. Upon seeing Perry's ships, Ryoma, who had been well aware of the West's power and technology, became concerned about Japan's future. He knew that the Western powers had conquered China earlier and he wanted to see them expelled from Japan by force.

He completed his training in 1856 at age 20 and returned to Tosa where he met with Kawada Shoryo. Kawada was renowned for his knowledge of Western culture and through him, Ryoma became familiar with Western politics, economy, and social systems. Shoryo was a samurai artist and scholar who had hand recorded in four brush-written volumes John Manjiro's (Nakahama Manjiro) account of being ship wrecked and taken to America aboard a whaling vessel. The account was the result of Manjiro's nine-month interrogation in 1852 by the Shogun's officials upon his return to Japan and subsequent arrest.

Nakahama Manjiro, like Sakamoto, was from the Tosa province. At age 14, he and four friends became shipwrecked while fishing and were picked up by an American whaling ship called the John Howland. Manjiro was taken to the United States where he studied English and navigation at the Oxford School in Fairhaven, Massachusetts.

On December 17, 1850, Manjiro and two of his friends set sail for Japan, reaching Okinawa on February 2, 1851. This was during Japan's period of isolation when Japanese citizens were forbidden to leave the country on penalty of death upon their return. Manjiro and his friends were taken into custody and questioned. Nine months later, they were released in Nagasaki and eventually returned to their homes in Tosa.

Manjiro was summoned to Edo in September of 1853 and made a *hatamoto* (a samurai in direct service to the Shogun). He served as an interpreter and translator for the Shogunate when Commodore Matthew Perry arrived in Japan. He was also instrumental in negotiating the Convention of Kanagawa, the first treaty between the United States and the Tokugawa Shogunate which ended Japan's 220-year period of national seclusion and opened her ports to trade with the West.

Commodore Matthew Calbraith Perry, a Freemason and member of The Holland Lodge No. 8 in New York since 1819, had commanded ships in several wars, including the War of 1812 and the Mexican-American War of 1846.

In 1852, United States President Millard Fillmore ordered Perry to force open Japanese ports to American trade through the use of gunboat diplomacy if necessary. Gunboat diplomacy was a term that came into existence during the nineteenth-century period of Western imperialism. The United States and Britain (primarily) would use their naval superiority to intimidate less powerful nations into granting concessions favorable to the Western powers.

Ironically, Fillmore was staunchly opposed to Freemasonry and was elected to the New York state legislature in 1828 on the Anti-masonic ticket.

Perry embarked from Norfolk, Virginia to Japan on November 24, 1852. He arrived in Naha (Okinawa) on May 17 of the following year and demanded an audience with the Ryukyuan ruler Sho Tai at Shuri Castle. Armed with secured promises that the Ryukyuan Kingdom would be open to trade with the United States, he journeyed to the Ogasawara Islands (also known as the Bonin Islands) located 620 miles (1,000 kilometers) south of Edo (Tokyo). Perry met with the local inhabitants and purchased a plot of land from them.

On July 8, 1853, Perry reached Uraga (a town in modern-day Kanagawa prefecture) located at the northern end of the Uraga Channel, a waterway connecting Edo Bay (Tokyo Bay) to the Sagami Gulf. He ordered his ships to sail toward Edo and turn their guns toward Uraga. He attempted to intimidate the Japanese by commanding his ships to fire blank shots from the 73 Paixhans shell guns they were equipped with. He landed in Kurihama (modern-day Yokosuka) on July 14, 1853 and presented the Japanese delegation with a letter given to him by President Fillmore. Perry departed for Hong Kong, with the promise that he would return the following year to hear Japan's response.

Commodore Perry returned to Japan on February 13, 1854, six months earlier than promised with ten ships and 1,600 men. The intention was to apply even more pressure on the Japanese to agree to his terms. Perry set foot on Japanese soil once again on March 8, 1854. On March 31, 1854, the Convention of Kanagawa was signed.

When Perry returned to the United States in 1855, he was awarded $20,000 (US$ 525,000 in 2018) in appreciation of his accomplishments in Japan.

Printed in the USA
CPSIA information can be obtained
at www.ICGtesting.com
JSHW020238120224
57161JS00001B/75